A DIFFERENT WORLD

A DIFFERENT WORLD

10 READY-TO-USE MEETINGS

Phil Bowyer

Authentic

11 10 09 08 07 06 05   7 6 5 4 3 2 1

First published 2005 by Authentic Media
9 Holdom Avenue, Bletchley,
Milton Keynes, Bucks, MK1 1QR, UK
and 129 Mobilization drive, Waynesboro, GA 30830-4575, USA
www.authenticmedia.co.uk

British Library Cataloguing in Publication Data
A catalogue record for this book is available from the British Library

ISBN 1-85078-652-6

Cover design by Sam Redwood
Cover photography by Geoff Crawford, Jim Loring,
Marcus Perkins and Mike Webb
Print Management by Adare Carwin
Printed by J.H. Haynes & Co., Sparkford

CONTENTS

WHAT'S ON THE CD-ROM?

Video: What is Poverty?

Global case studies: Bangladesh, Tanzania, Ugandan child soldiers, Burundi, London, Southampton, Glasgow, Kent, Cambodia, Zambia, Brazil, Sierra Leone, India, Uganda

Printables: 'Just' war, 'Just' arms, Postcard, HIV and AIDS, The molecule game, COST, Interest free?, Trade rules, Tsunami 2004, Disaster game, Sponsor form, The poverty gap, Whole hearted, The Micah Call

Worksheets: Welcome sheets, Every second counts, How debt happened, The cost of aid

Interactive presentation: Aid-Adder

Drama: Food and drink, Debt

Photos: Pictures of poverty

ACKNOWLEDGEMENTS

Particular thanks to those people who have contributed specific content to the various sessions throughout this resource: Steve Adams, Craig Borlase, Tara Devlin, Geoff Harley-Mason, Nigel Roberts, Esther Stansfield, David Westlake and Helen Wilkinson.

Thanks also to James Alexander, Andy Baldwin, Rachel Bowyer, Seren Boyd, Alison Brown, Lorna Duddy, Bryan Evans, Mari Griffith, Sophie Harding, Zoë Hayes, Dewi Hughes, Annie Kirke, Veena O'Sullivan, Sarah La Trobe and Laura Webster for all your ideas, input and inspiration.

HOW TO USE THIS RESOURCE EFFECTIVELY

WHAT'S DONE FOR YOU...

INTRODUCTION

Before each session starts, a short introduction provides you with some background information to put the issue in context.

SESSION PLANS

Each session has one or more of the following elements: activities and games to help get your group thinking about the issue; a Bible passage to be looked at and discussed; a prayer about the issues raised; a chance for input from you; and a response section to challenge the group to do something about it. The following icons will guide you through the sessions:

A DIFFERENT WAY

Action is an important aspect of this resource, which is why each session concludes with a response to what has been discussed. This action is in the form of a local, national and global response. As group facilitator it is your role to decide which of these is most appropriate for your group – of course you could do them all! Some actions should be encouraged within the session itself, and other responses during the days, weeks, months and years to follow.

ON THE CD-ROM

The CD-ROM contains a range of resources to accompany the sessions. These include worksheets, case studies, dramas, printable photographs, interactive presentations and video footage. They are referenced using the session number, then the letter A, B, C, etc., and then the type of resource. For example, the first resource in session 1 is called Resource 1A: Photos.

WHAT YOU'LL NEED TO DO...

READY TO USE OR READY TO CHOOSE?

These sessions may be ready to use but that doesn't mean you won't have to prepare for them in advance. You may need to collect some additional resources, so don't leave it all until 7.05 p.m. when your group is due to arrive at 8.00 p.m. No resource will work 'off the shelf' with every group. You are the expert on what sort of people will be there. Read the material and adapt it; you know what will best suit, teach and challenge your group. Depending on how long you meet for, you may find you have more material than you need. Don't worry; this was a conscious decision taken when compiling the resource – better to have too much than too little. Be wise about how you choose what to keep and what to lose from each session. Ask yourself about the needs of your group and how each individual activity may help or hinder your progress.

A GUIDE KNOWS THE WAY

These sessions are designed to challenge your group members. We all find changing our attitudes and behaviour difficult. You need to have read the sessions and considered the issues yourself before you lead your group through them. Remember that each session plan begins with some brief background reading that is for your benefit. You may need to pray about your own attitudes when God prompts you to change. If this happens you will be in a strong position to challenge the group.

WHAT GOD CAN DO...

A Different World is all about changing people's attitudes and behaviour towards the poor. Your responsibility is to bring your group into contact with God and His values. That's why you share your life with them and teach them what God has said in the Bible. It is then the job of the Holy Spirit to encourage people to see whether there is a need to change.

So do be confident:

● in God

● in the Bible

● in your material, which you have worked hard to prepare.

Don't worry about:

● having to win the argument

● needing to see immediate results.

Do remember to:

● pray for your group

● pray that God will convict people to change

● think of ways to help your group to respond to what they have learned – the concluding part of each session entitled *A Different Way* will be particularly important here.

WHAT ELSE YOU CAN DO...

● **Get feedback.** If you want your group to shout out suggestions, first get them into small groups to think things through and ask them to appoint a spokesperson to give feedback.

● **Extra research.** Before your session and once you have prepared, do some extra research. Try websites to get some additional up-to-date info on the subject.

● **Visuals.** Think of some visuals that would be useful to set the scene. These could be pictures or objects that you could collect beforehand.

● **Grill an expert.** Have a think about somebody, either in your group or wider community, who may have some first-hand knowledge or experience of the issues and invite them along.

● **Stuff.** Always have the following to hand in case of emergency: A4 paper; some pens (that work); large sheets of paper; marker pens; reusable sticky pads; a portable CD player – appropriate music in the background can help to create a relaxed atmosphere. Try to use instrumental music as a background to prayer.

● **Your own life.** Think about how you can bring your own experiences into what you are talking about.

INTRODUCTION
POVERTY – NOW YOU SEE IT?

For the LORD your God is God of gods and Lord of lords, the great God, mighty and awesome...

Before you turn over, think about what kind of images spring to mind when you read this verse from Deuteronomy 10:17.

HOW GOD SEES IT

You probably have images of a great big God looking down on the world from the heavens. Perhaps you saw endless stars, multiple planets and all kind of massive impressive feats of his creation engineering. But read the verse which follows on: 'He defends the cause of the fatherless and the widow, and loves the alien, giving him food and clothing' (Deut. 10:18).

Now what are you thinking? It's truly amazing: the God who flung the planets into place, whose fingers put the stars into space, is the same God who raises his hand to say enough is enough, whose arm gathers and comforts the foreigner, whose palms pour out plenty for the sake of the needy. Our God is not some kind of giant toy-maker who after taking great care in making us, simply winds us up and then leaves us to it to wind down in whatever way we see fit. Our God gets involved and continues to care. And he calls us to get involved and to care for others in the same way that he does.

HOW IT IS

- A child dies every 15 seconds from water-related diseases.[1]

- In the next minute, five people will die of AIDS and ten people will join more than 40 million others who are infected with HIV.[2]

- The poorest countries in the world have debts totalling $523 billion, and pay $100 million to the rich world EVERY DAY.[3]

- The people who make your clothes earn as little as £4 for a six-day week, working 13-hour shifts, and have no rights to speak out about it.[4]

- Nine hundred thousand children needlessly died last month owing to causes associated with extreme poverty.[5]

- In 2004 there was a total of 17.1 million refugees and asylum seekers worldwide.[6]

- During the last decade more than two million children are estimated to have died as a direct result of armed conflict; another six million have been seriously injured or permanently disabled, many of them by landmines.[7]

- Over the last 50 years, the number of natural disasters occurring worldwide has more than doubled, from 350 per year in the early nineties to over 750 – and it's poor people who suffer the most.[8]

HOW WE SEE IT

Learning about disasters through the media is probably the point at which most people first begin to see something of the reality of what it means to live in a different world. Regardless of whether these are 'one off' disasters, such as earthquakes or floods, or some of the world's ongoing struggles, such as famine, conflict and the HIV and AIDS pandemic, they often bring about periods of national shock, reflection and an openness to do things differently. Whether through our words or our actions, disasters can provide real opportunities for us to influence policies and practices, which we hope, in the future, may reduce the vulnerability and poverty of real people. As Christians we ought to be doing everything possible to grab opportunities like these with both hands. Emergency disaster relief may provide amazing opportunities to bring hope to situations of despair, but in doing so we need to be equally aware of ways in which we can begin to reduce the impact of whatever dangers people living in poverty may face in the future. Seeing a way to address poverty has to happen on a number of different levels:

- **Locally:** The best way to do this is by understanding and supporting community development or transformation projects and programmes that exist to respond to the long-term needs of people living in poverty. To have any real impact on poverty it is the poor who need to be enabled to start influencing their own circumstances. Organizations such as Tearfund see it as their priority to make sure that local churches realize their potential and become the significant force for community transformation that they should be. By partnering with local community initiatives Tearfund recognizes the impact the poor can have on local, national and global situations that affect them most. In summary Tearfund believes that:

Unless the poor are empowered to speak for themselves within their local structures and context, their real needs and priorities are likely to go unheard or be misrepresented. Conversely, empowering the poor to speak for themselves by building their confidence, knowledge and access to institutions of power, enables them to represent their own needs within national and international political processes and demand greater transparency and pro-poor policies.[9]

- **Nationally:** Whatever the degree of positive change that is able to take place at grass-roots local level, decisions made nationally will always impact the poorest people the most. Something as serious as a national decision to engage in conflict will inevitably force a great number of people into poverty, displacing them from productive land and denying or destroying what few assets they have. Reducing the causes of conflict through Christian mediation and campaigning for greater justice will significantly reduce poverty. Of course the degree to which a government is committed to ridding itself of poverty through good government is a critical factor in overcoming poverty and vulnerability.

- **Globally:** Some of the factors that contribute to people's poverty are the result of decisions by international organizations that are not part of any particular country.[10] Trade, aid and debt are all issues that impact the poor greatly but which they generally have little control over. Trade represents one of the greatest sources of potential income to the world's poor, but with relatively unfair trade rules they rarely see the benefit. International rules tend to be dictated by the policies and practices of richer countries. Changing these practices naturally requires some form of international advocacy work either by the poorer countries themselves or by other agencies on their behalf.

- **All of the above:** Of course many of the factors which contribute to poverty need action on every level if we are to see any real positive impact for the poor. Climate change is just one of a number of poverty issues that demands an international response as well as local action. It's the millions of poor people in the world who are most affected by the way we continue to exploit the earth's resources. International strategies to reduce the impact of climate change also need to be supported by effective local implementation. This brings us back neatly to where we started: national and local action against poverty.

HOW WE SHOULD BE

Whatever your motivation in life, surely it's hard to look at the facts of world poverty without feeling some kind of urge to do something about it. The verses from Deuteronomy 10 with which we began this introduction to poverty reveal a little about who God is, and even what he does, but read further and you'll discover that his words go on to leave us with a challenge all of our own:

- Who God is: 'For the LORD your God is God of gods and Lord of lords, the great God, mighty and awesome...' (Deut. 10:17)

- What he does: 'He defends the cause of the fatherless and the widow, and loves the alien, giving him food and clothing.' (Deut. 10:18)

- What he requires of us: 'And *you* are to love those who are aliens...' (Deut. 10:19)

Regardless of whether it's the lonely, a stranger or the hungry, it seems we too have some responsibility towards those in need. The fact that the three verses here in Deuteronomy are a repetition of a similar pattern of events just three verses earlier in verses 14–16 suggests that this is something God really wants his people to hear. Most of us probably have some idea of who God is, what he does, and maybe even what he asks of us. The question we're probably most unsure about is 'how?' This resource is designed to enable you to take a closer look at eight key aspects of global poverty. It contains plenty of opportunities for you and your group to understand what it means to live in a different world and to find ways for you to respond to its needs at local, national, global, and, of course, a personal level.

SESSION 1
WHAT IS POVERTY?

Aim: To understand the ways in which we can step in and change people's circumstances, breaking the cycle of poverty which traps people and keeps them poor.

You will need: *Resource 1A: Photos*, sticky notes, pens, large sheets of paper, enough balls of coloured wool for each individual, stapler, staples, reusable sticky pads, *Resource 1B: Video*, Bibles, flip chart paper, marker pens.

Pictures of poverty (10 mins)

Use a selection of photographs from *Resource 1A: Photos* to begin to think through what people feel when they see images of poverty. Print off the photos, place them on the floor, and ask each individual to look through the selection and choose one that particularly strikes them. You could use the following explanations of the photos to get them thinking about the people and their situations.

PEOPLE AND POVERTY

HAND IN HAND Her grandmother holds her hand, but 13-year-old Gia faces a future without parents. Every 14 seconds a child is orphaned by AIDS. Tearfund supports many projects in the fight against HIV and AIDS, showing Christian compassion in great suffering. ⟶ *GOD'S WORLD*

BABY IN HAMMOCK A Chaco Indian baby in Argentina. Tearfund helps indigenous people maintain their way of life. Traditional skills provide alternative sources of income. ⟶ *GOD'S WORLD*

AFGHAN REFUGEES WITH BOWLS Afghan refugee children in the Akora Khattack camp, Pakistan. Tearfund's Disaster Response Teams and local partners bring rapid relief to devastated communities. *GOD'S WORLD*

CHILDREN AT BAMBOO DOOR Burmese children peep through the door of their nursery school. Changing a child's life through education means transforming the future for a whole community. *GOD'S WORLD*

CHILDREN JUMPING INTO FLOOD WATER Cambodian children at play. Water is one of the most valuable assets for any community, and Tearfund's *Water Matters* campaign aims to halve the number of people without access to safe water and sanitation by 2015. *GOD'S WORLD*

Spend some time reflecting on the photos and then hand out a pile of sticky notes to each person, asking them to write on each separate note one word that comes into their head when they see their image. (With larger numbers, try sticking the images to a wall and ask people to move around the room and reflect on each for a few minutes.) Questions that might help them think could include:

● What does it mean to be poor?

● How would it feel?

● What might you lack?

● What might you need?

● How might your health be?

If people are finding it hard, encourage them to pray about the situations and ask God to reveal his feelings about what they're seeing. They should stick the sticky notes onto, or close to, the relevant photo. Allow time for feedback once you feel people have finished.

● ●

What is Poverty? (5 mins)

Open up and play *Resource 1B: Video*. Ask people which elements of poverty in particular struck them. Discuss in what ways this was similar to or different from their thoughts during the opening exercise. Organizations such as Tearfund that are involved in community development work recognize the following as causes of poverty:

● **Lack of Empowerment** due to a lack of social assets such as good governance, family networks and education, resulting in a lack of individual confidence to articulate views and needs, lack of political voice and the repression of civil liberties, including the right to express a faith.

● **Lack of Opportunity** to obtain vital assets, such as land, tools or credit, through individual effort or public services, or to use them to generate wealth or well being.

● **Lack of Security** due to the sudden loss of life, assets or opportunity through natural disasters like hurricanes or drought or human-made disasters such as war or economic collapse.

Poverty trap (15 mins)

Take three chairs and place them as far apart as the room in which you meet allows you to. On each chair write one of the following titles:

- Lack of Empowerment
- Lack of Opportunity
- Lack of Security

Encourage your group to take the sticky notes from the previous exercise and place them on the chair that they feel best fits in terms of what they feel may have led to this element of poverty. This exercise is not designed as a test, but as a challenge to enable your group to think about poverty in more depth – there are no wrong answers as such.

Hand everyone one ball of different coloured wool and ask them to walk around the room visiting each one of the three stations at random. As they do so they need to be looking for factors which they think may be linked to others on either of the other two chairs. Once they find links they need to wrap their wool around the chair leg, or back, and move on to another station to find another related factor.

You should finish the activity with a visual web of the connections that show just how difficult it must be for people to escape from the trap that is poverty. One area inevitably reinforces another: it's very difficult to weaken the trap.

HELPFUL HINT

Poverty cycle

On a very simple level, if you are poor in a developing country you are more likely to

- be unable to afford decent housing
- which means you may be forced to live in slum conditions
- disease is probably more evident here
- you are more likely to become sick
- because you are ill, you cannot get work
- without work you will have no access to money to buy medicine so you don't get better
- this means you have even less chance of working or affording decent housing...

And so the cycle continues. If you are fortunate enough to have children, they may be able to work to help supplement your income, but in these conditions they, too, are just as likely to fall sick as you, so that income is lost, too. You would like to break the cycle for your children, but you cannot afford to send them to school so they are unable to get better jobs and so the cycle goes on from generation to generation.

Poverty cycle (15 mins)

The following exercise may help your group to go beyond superficial answers to causes of poverty to uncover more fundamental issues. 'But why?' flow charts are a way of helping people to think about the root causes of problems. They're also a good way of challenging assumptions and prejudices. Split into groups and ask each group to choose one issue of poverty – you may choose to use each of those highlighted on the video (*Resource 1B*) or something that came out of the 'Pictures of poverty' exercise. In groups:

● Ask yourself the question: 'Why does this situation exist?'

● After each answer, ask again: 'But why?'

● Keep asking the question until you have got as far as you think you can go, for example:

There are so many asylum seekers

▼

But why?

▼

Because they've left their own country

▼

But why?

▼

For fear of losing their lives

▼

But why?

▼

Because their community is being persecuted

▼

But why?

▼

Because of their beliefs

▼

But why?

▼

Because they are different from those with the most power

▼

... and so on

HELPFUL HINT

More complicated issues are best represented through a flow chart, because there are multiple answers to any one 'But why?' question. This exercise is intended to over-simplify the issues of poverty. The sessions that follow in this book will look at some of the questions it raises in more depth.

If you take this exercise to its extreme you may find that some groups' only conclusion to the question of 'But Why?' is 'The Fall'. They may be closer to the truth than they realize.

The cause and the effect (5 mins)

A Christian approach to recognizing the causes that work together to sustain the 'poverty trap' ought to include one more factor: **Lack of Relationship**. Human beings were created by God to live in relationship with their Creator, other individuals, their community and the earth. As a result of our broken relationship with God there is a tendency for all other relationships to be broken too. Doing our own thing, rather than God's, impacts the whole of human life. Label it as 'sin' if you like, but it's basically a series of bad choices and not God choices that are the ultimate cause of poverty.

The poor are not poor because of their own sins but often because of factors beyond their control that are perpetuated by the unjust choices of others. They are stuck in a seemingly endless cycle of sin that is rooted in oppressive political, economic and religious structures. The poor lack *power, opportunity* and *security* because the rich claim too much for themselves. Unless the rich and powerful take responsibility and begin to address the various ways they abuse their power, then little progress will be made in reducing the levels of poverty.

POVERTY – A DIFFERENT WAY...

As long as secular development models don't acknowledge that there is a need to address sin as a result of relationship meltdown (expressed by greed, envy, prejudice, and so on) in order to break the poverty cycle, then they will remain incomplete. Ultimately it is faith in Jesus that restores our relationship with God and it is through this that our recognition of our need to restore relationships with others becomes even more obvious.

Globally – will there always be poor among us? (10 mins)

As long as humankind's relationship with God remains dysfunctional, the Bible says there will always be the poor (Deut. 15:11). That ought not act as an excuse for not taking action for and with people who are living in poverty, but rather a stimulus to do something to make things better. Select some or all of the following verses and ask your group to discuss the similarities and then the differences between the verses. Sort them into verses that demonstrate that the poor can be helped:

● By others upholding justice – Ps. 82:3; Deut. 24:12–15; Prov. 22:22; Is. 10:1–12; Jer. 22:16

● With gifts – Acts 10:4; Deut. 15:7–8; Ps. 112:9; Prov. 31:20; Mt. 19:21; Lk. 19:8; Eph. 4:28; 1 Tim. 6:17–18

● In practical ways – Mt. 25:34–40; Lk. 11:41; 1 Tim. 5:9–10; Jas. 2:15–16; 1 Jn. 3:17

BIBLICAL BACKGROUND
You may find it interesting to note the different ways in which we're called to respond to the poor in the Old and New Testaments. While the Old Testament focuses on how we ought to care for the poor, Jesus's priority shifts almost entirely to warning us of the danger of wealth and the responsibility we have to use what we have in order to bless others. Jesus underlines the fact that greed leading to injustice is a fundamental cause of poverty.

The key to any relationship, whether it's maintained locally, nationally or globally, is a growing understanding of the issues which matter to any one individual, group or community. Recognizing where you are and where you need to be in order to able to step in and make a difference is crucial. Finish this session with a time of reflection and prayer. Ask yourself where you are now and where you want to be, in terms of:

● your relationship with your God

● your relationship with your group

● your relationship with your different world.

Record your thoughts on a postcard, stuff it into a self addressed envelope and revisit it once you've complete this material.

THE DIFFERENT ISSUES...
CLIMATE CHANGE

Over recent years we have made huge strides forward in terms of technology. Many of these innovations require power in order for them to work. Whether it's your mobile phone, wireless connection or portable stereo, it's sometimes easy to forget that they all require energy to operate. Even the convenience food we eat uses up energy in the way it is packaged, processed and transported. This energy may be readily available and relatively cheap, but have you ever thought about the hidden cost?

The more we need and use energy, the more the world's temperature rises. Greenhouse gases produced by human activity, such as carbon dioxide (CO_2) and methane, are raising global temperatures and causing harmful climate change. The majority of global warming over the last few years can be attributed to human behaviour. Three-quarters of the carbon dioxide added to the atmosphere during the last 20 years comes from the burning of fossil fuels (coal, oil, natural gas). Huge forests, which once absorbed CO_2, are disappearing to make way for more lucrative industry. The earth's natural recycling system – plants changing carbon dioxide into oxygen – is being destroyed daily. As we put pressure on the global ecosystem, the way we live affects the climate.

The natural consequence of living as we do is a rise in global temperatures and the associated rising sea levels. Global average surface temperatures have increased by 0.6 °C during the last century; a rise of up to 5.8 °C is predicted by 2100 if climate change continues at its current rate.[11] Mountain glaciers are retreating and there is a 40 percent decline in Arctic sea-ice thickness.[12] Both are important in reflecting the sun's energy back to space. Warmer weather results in a rise in sea levels; levels have already risen 0.2 metres and are forecast to rise by 0.4 metres by 2080.[13] Climate change contributes to the extreme weather conditions in the form of floods, hurricanes, droughts and heatwaves that we are beginning to see more regularly, not only overseas but also in the UK. And they're on the increase. In the 1990s we saw 87 natural disasters compared with just 20 in the 1950s.[14]

People living in poorer communities are the most vulnerable to such dramatic changes in climate. A slum community on a riverbank is more vulnerable when flooding occurs than a prosperous Western town with well-built brick houses, flood defences and sophisticated early warning systems. People in poorer countries in Africa, Asia and Latin America who are often most affected by complex climatic conditions have the least capacity to respond.

PEOPLE AND POVERTY

Here are a few natural disasters from recent times:

October 1998: HONDURAS AND NICARAGUA

Hurricane Mitch blasted through Honduras and Nicaragua killing 11,000 and leaving three million people dependent on aid.

February 2000: MOZAMBIQUE

A tropical cyclone ravaged Mozambique. One million were left homeless and hundreds were swept away.

October 2000: BANGLADESH

Floods claimed the lives of hundreds and left two million people homeless.

August 2001: AFGHANISTAN

Five million Afghans faced starvation after three years of drought.

Source: Tearfund

Perhaps it's time we showed a little more respect for our global environment. We need to think about the energy we use and change how we live. We need to reduce the energy we use to slow down climate change. We have a personal responsibility to become part of the solution. Despite our incredible technological advances, we haven't managed so far to find a way to control the climate, but we can affect it. As individuals, families, businesses and churches, there are ways in which we can reduce our greenhouse gas emissions.

SESSION 2
CLIMATE CHANGE

Aim: To show how climate change impacts the poor. To understand the impact our lifestyle choices have upon climate change and to think through ways in which we can have an impact on the climate in this country and overseas.

You will need: Selection of old clothes, thermometer, bucket, selection of fruit of various sizes, ice cubes, Quavers crisps, crackers, glass of water, *Resource 2A: Case study*, Bibles, pens, paper, cardboard, plastic sheeting, mats and wooden poles, a bag of rubbish, enough pairs of rubber gloves for each individual.

Preparation: In the week leading up to your session, save all your rubbish in a bag (preferably washed and cleaned!).

It's life, but not as it should be (30 mins)

Before you consider how climate change happens and the implications it has for our lives and the lives of those living in poverty, use each of the following activities to introduce some of the key ways climate change is affecting our world. Set up three 'weather' stations with the following activities:

HOTTER

Get hold of as many old clothes as you can. Split into teams and ask each team to select a volunteer. They are to dress their volunteer in as many clothes as they can. The winner is the person with the most clothes on (or, if you have a thermometer, the hottest). Another option would be to split your group into smaller groups and ask people to build the highest tower out of their own clothes, e.g. socks, shoes, coats, scarves, etc.

> ### FACE FACTS
>
> Global average surface temperatures have increased by 0.6°C in the last century.[15]

WETTER

Fill a bucket with water and ask people to 'bob' for increasingly difficult-to-grab floating foodstuffs, starting with a strawberry and ending with a melon. Or split into smaller groups and see who can stack ice cubes the highest, and for the longest. (Revisit this one at the end of the session.)

FACE FACTS

Global average sea levels have risen by up to 0.2 metres.[16] Heavy precipitation events in the Northern Hemisphere have increased by up to 4 percent.[17]

DRIER

Hand out a Quaver crisp to each person, ask them to place it on their tongue and see who can keep it 'alive' in their mouth the longest. Alternatively, try a game of consuming crackers – the person who can eat the most without the need of a drink of water is the winner.

FACE FACTS

Those areas already experiencing drought will be subject to an increased frequency and intensity of such events. In fact, all weather extremes will intensify.

Move on to think through some of the reasons our world is changing through climate change. Take feedback on the different elements the games covered if you feel it's appropriate.

● ●

Why does the forecast look so bleak? (5 mins)

Over recent years an ever-increasing number of 'natural' disasters have been shaking the planet. Scientists acknowledge that these are just one consequence of climate change. Most global warming observed over the last 50 years is attributable to human activities. Carbon dioxide (CO_2) is the main gas causing what is known as a greenhouse effect: when the sun's heat is trapped on its return journey into space. Whilst burning coal, oil and natural gas leads to dense CO_2 emissions in the atmosphere, the vegetation that once removed this (replacing it with oxygen) is rapidly being removed – 80 percent of the world's original forests has been destroyed.[18] Other greenhouse gases such as methane (produced by cattle, rice agriculture, fossil fuel use and landfills) and nitrous oxide (produced by the chemical industry, cattle feed lots and agricultural soils) are all factors in causing the change in climate.

Discuss recent disasters that you are aware of that you feel may have been caused by changes in our climate.

Who pays, we decide (10 mins)

The poor have the least money to adapt and prepare for climate change. Around 96 percent of all deaths from natural disasters occur in developing countries.[19] The Kyoto Protocol is an international treaty designed to make sure industrialized countries reduce their use of fossil fuels. Countries have been asked to make a 5 percent emission reduction from 1990 levels by the period 2008–2012.[20] This is insignificant compared to the 60 percent reduction needed to stabilize CO_2 atmospheric concentrations.[21] Consider the following case study (*Resource 2A: Case study*).

PEOPLE AND POVERTY

CASE STUDY – BANGLADESH

Nur Mohammed lives in a dangerous place. His house has been swept away at least twice in recent years. Storms and fierce currents are biting huge chunks out of the island where he lives – Hatiya Island, off the south coast of Bangladesh – and it's getting worse. Nur Mohammed says: 'The island is breaking up faster than before. There are big storms more often. The place where we used to live is now at least a kilometre (0.6 miles) out to sea.'

Climate change is not just a remote scientific theory. The world is getting hotter, and like a person with a temperature, it's showing signs of sickness. Even the UK has seen freak weather recently. The 1990s saw 87 natural disasters, compared to 20 in the 1950s. The world's leading scientists are predicting more extreme weather, more floods, more droughts, and worse storms. High intensity hurricanes such as those experienced by the USA in 2005, and storms such as Hurricane Mitch, which killed more than 11,000 people in Central America in 1998, can be expected to occur more often.

It's the poor that suffer more than any of us. Lack of choice means they often live in dangerous places that are vulnerable to disasters. Bangladesh is particularly vulnerable because it's a delta for some of Asia's biggest rivers. Erosion is getting worse as more and more water and floods pour down the rivers into the sea. Most of Bangladesh is less than a couple of metres above sea level. Global average sea levels have already risen by 0.2 metres. If this continues, millions of people in Bangladesh and other low-lying areas will lose their homes and land.

Source: *Lifesaver: Swept away*, Tearfund

Isn't it time we stopped living as if the planet belonged just to us? As Christians, we must take up the challenge of living on God's earth God's way. To make our own lifestyle choices for the benefit of people and planet, and to encourage politicians to act to eradicate poverty in a way that protects the environment.

To let? (15 mins)

Read Genesis chapter 1 together. Using a large sheet of wallpaper lining, divided into seven sections or columns, ask your group to draw or paint pictures of each of the different elements of God's creation as described in Genesis 1. Spend some time reflecting on the wonder, the variety and the abundance of creativity we can see in God's world.

Now take the images and rip off those which you feel may be under threat due to the way we live our lives

---

HELPFUL HINT

Notice whether any individuals choose men or women for their 'endangered list' – which, of course, for the reasons outlined throughout this session, they ought to.

Discuss how God's creation looks now and how you feel about the things *you've* 'created' being destroyed. In what ways does that give you an insight into how God might feel about *his* creation being destroyed?

Discuss your understanding of the words 'subdue', 'rule' and 'give' (vv. 28–30). How do these relate to our role in creation?

BIBLICAL BACKGROUND

Whether humankind is the dominant species in creation is not in question here – i.e. we are what God said we would be. The point is not that we have dominion but how we exercise it.

Reflect once more on the 'Let there be...' verses in the passage. Ask the group to consider how God must feel about the fact that some of our thoughtless everyday *choices* directly oppose what are, in effect, his *commandments* for life. Who are we to think that our need to 'do' overrides God's intention for his creation to 'be'?

Discuss some of the ways we choose to disobey God's commands through our everyday lifestyle choices.

Finally consider why the writers of the Bible thought it was significant to mention the fact that God rested. What does this mean for us, for others, and for God's creation? List some ideas about how our lifestyle could provide more opportunities for 'rest'.

CLIMATE – A DIFFERENT WAY...

Globally – a place of 'refuge'

Why not turn where you meet, i.e. your church or your home, into a flood shelter and arrange a sleepover? Perhaps encourage your wider church to have a weekend of focusing on climate too. Start by building your own house. You'll need: cardboard, plastic sheeting, mats and wooden poles. Divide into small groups of three or four and ask each to try to build a small shelter. If possible – and if the weather is good – you could build these outside and see which ones last the longest when exposed to the weather! You can point out that this is exactly the sort of housing that very poor people live in – some because they are very poor, and others because they have lost their normal house in a disaster.

PEOPLE AND POVERTY

Tearfund's Disaster Management Team (DMT) has been delivering support and relief to those in areas susceptible to natural disasters for over a decade. Christian partners supported by Tearfund are also helping people living in vulnerable communities to prepare for disasters. They strengthen their houses, help them grow more food and discuss what to do in times of emergency.

Afghanistan: The DMT has been working here on and off since 1996, yet recently the work has been disrupted due to the alarming increase in the level of insecurity throughout the country. Work in some parts has been suspended, but the DMT continues to provide those living in camps in the South with water, sanitation, schooling and health education. Tearfund partners are busy building roads, installing latrines and providing health and education facilities. One partner is helping recently returned refugees to become more financially independent, while another has built and fully stocked a number of schools.

Ethiopia: Tearfund partners have helped tens of thousands of people survive crippling droughts. The Meserete Kristos Church (MKC) distributes seeds to the worst affected families as well running a cash-for-work project in areas where there is still food available to buy. Some 6000 participants are working on projects such as building dams and improving roads. Participants can buy food and other essentials with their wages.

Southern Africa: Southern Africa's drought kick-started a massive reaction from Tearfund supporters, who gave £5.5 million in 2002's appeal, which touched more than one million lives in Zambia, Zimbabwe, Malawi and Angola. Rural families worked on community projects with 16 Tearfund partner agencies in exchange for maize, seeds or fertilizer. Improved farming methods were also taught, making the future look brighter for generations to come.

Source: Tearfund

Spend some time in the shelter. Add any questions, thoughts and prayers to the 'walls' on the inside.

Thank God that he offers refuge to everyone, whether they're poor or rich, and that he promises to save us if we believe in Jesus. Pray for the people of countries such as Bangladesh as they prepare to face bad floods that may come any time. Ask whether individuals in your group, school, family or church have relations or friends overseas, or support people who work overseas. Pray for them. In what ways is climate change impacting their lives? Pray for each other or those you know who are going through difficult times, that God will be close to them.

• •

Locally – as easy as ABC

Making a positive impact on climate change starts at home, starts with you. It's simpler than you think. Think about the following:

A IS FOR ALTERNATIVE USE OF ENERGY

Using energy efficiently can dramatically reduce greenhouse gas emissions and can therefore reduce the impact of climate change. As a group, discuss ways to make your home, school, church or college more energy-efficient. If it helps, think about the different ways you use energy throughout the day, for example:

- **Put** on an extra jumper and turn down the heating – just one degree lower can reduce fuel consumption by 10 percent.[22]

- **Wash** your clothes at lower temperatures – there is no need to wash clothes above 40 °C.

- **Switch** off your TV, PC or stereo – even when they're on standby, some models still use 40–70 percent of the energy they use when switched on.[23]

- **Unplug** your laptop or mobile phone once they're fully charged – not only does it save energy, but it also prolongs the life of your battery.

- **Use** low-energy light bulbs – they use 80 percent less electricity and last 8–15 times longer than standard bulbs.

- **Shut** the fridge door during your midnight snack – for each minute it's open it takes three minutes of energy to cool it down again.[24]

If you can't use the washer or don't know how to control the heating, ask someone who does and can – ignorance is no excuse for lack of action. It's essential that individuals, groups and businesses adopt as many of these measures as possible at personal and local levels. However, both at national and international level, governments also have responsibility to make 'sustainable' choices easy through providing and supporting viable alternatives and incentives.

FACE FACTS

- Simply by not being efficient, UK households waste £96 million worth of energy every week, an average of £200 per household per year.[25]

- In the UK, around 25 percent of all CO_2 emissions released into the atmosphere come from the energy used to run our homes – that's six tonnes of CO_2 every year![26]

- Every year two tonnes of CO_2 is released into the atmosphere when we buy electricity from 'dirty' electricity generators, i.e. ones that burn oil, coal or gas to generate energy.[27]

Renewable energy and energy efficient technology can play important roles in mitigating climate change. Since CO_2 is the main cause of global warming, switching to a 'green' electricity provider will help to slow the process of climate change. The recognition of the potential of wind, biomass, wave, tidal, hydropower and solar technology to reduce dependence on fossil fuels is increasing. Don't think it's someone else's responsibility; you use it too, so it's just as much your choice as it is the bill payers![28]

B IS FOR BETTER USE OF ENERGY

The UK currently recycles just 8 percent of its household waste, even though 70 percent of the waste in our dustbins can be recycled![29] Around 80 percent of the rubbish we throw away in the UK goes straight into landfill sites, which, as well as emitting CO_2, are also the second largest source of methane emissions.[30] Recycling our waste is just one way to cut back on the amount of rubbish destined for landfills and incineration, and thereby reducing the greenhouse gases they emit.[31] Get hold of a bag of rubbish (a week's worth should be enough) and ask your group to sort through the rubbish to find which bits they think can and can't be recycled. They should then work this out as a percentage of the total waste and discuss ways they could improve on this.

HELPFUL HINT

Rather than a landfill, almost a third of domestic waste could go straight onto the compost heap.[32] Try turning your food scraps and tea bags into compost and return the nutrients and energy back to the soil where they can be reused. Contact your local council for details of local composting schemes.

Your local council may also offer a kerbside recycling service for non-organic waste, so why not give them a call. Find out where your nearest recycling banks are by visiting www.recycle-more.co.uk.

C IS FOR CUTTING USE OF ENERGY

Cutting consumption is the best way to tackle climate change. The rate at which our levels of consumption are increasing is simply not sustainable. Whether this consumption requires the use of fossil fuels or other 'green' technology, the more we consume, the more of the earth's resources we require and the more harmful waste we produce. Return to your bag of rubbish, and this time ask your group to sort through it and work out which waste can and can't be reused or reduced, for example:

● **Reuse** things rather than throwing them in the bin. Reuse paper and envelopes by sticking labels over the address. Buy rechargeable items, such as batteries and cameras, instead of disposable ones. Take your old clothes and books to charity shops. We use around ten billion plastic bags every year in the UK, most of which end up in landfill sites and take 500 years to decompose.[33]

● **Reduce** the amount of energy you waste. Stop unwanted junk mail being sent to you – register at the Mailing Preference Service at www.mpsonline.org.uk or call 020 7291 3310. Reduce the number of plastic bags you use – get a fabric bag or reusable bag.

HELPFUL HINT

PLANES, TRAINS AND AUTOMOBILES

Of course it's not just household waste that we need to cut in order to reduce our negative impact on the climate. Transport in the UK is the fastest growing source of CO_2, accounting for about one quarter of our total emissions.[34] Your group may not yet own their own transport but they will benefit from it in one form or another. Here are a few tips on transport to think through:

● As a result of the growth in budget European airlines, and the increasingly popularity of short overseas breaks, greenhouse gas pollution due to air travel is increasing. Reducing short-haul trips, which are more environmentally polluting per passenger kilometre than longer trips, is one way we can positively affect climate change. If you do have to fly it is possible to offset your emissions by donating to organizations who will plant trees, invest in renewable energy and research into energy efficiency on your behalf.[35]

● Taking the train for shorter trips will cut down on pollution. In fact, for shorter trips public transport in general is less damaging to the environment than cars are.

● If you can't use public transport, car sharing is a good alternative. Joining friends to and from school or on a night out will make a real difference. Walking is even better: it not only reduces pollution but could also save you money. Trips to the local shop, going to church, getting to football practice or travelling to school could all provide great walking opportunities. Cycling is also good news for slowing climate change and it keeps you fit.[36]

Tearfund's *For tomorrow's world too* has lots more suggestions on how you can cut your personal contribution to climate change. To order your free copy call 0845 355 8355 (ROI 0044 845 355 8355).

● ●

Nationally – words and pictures

If we are going to see a shift in the political outlook on climate change we need to turn up the heat at Downing Street. Pray for each of the countries you know that are experiencing the effects of climate change, and for people in disaster-prone poor countries, then create a pile of post at Number 10 Downing Street. Discuss creative ways of reminding the Prime Minster that we need to take action. The more creative ways we can use to remind the Prime Minster that we need to take action for the better. Here are a few ideas to get you started:

● **Words**: Write a letter to tell the Prime Minister about the lifestyle changes that you've already committed to. Include a recent newspaper article about global warming, or why not recycle a receipt, or even the paper packaging of something you have purchased to make your lifestyle more energy efficient. Send it as evidence of the things you have done to reduce your contribution to climate change.

● **Pictures**: Take a photograph of some examples of the lifestyle changes you've committed to, for example your cycle route or your walk to college, or things you have done to make your home more energy efficient. Get the children from your church or local schools involved in some creative campaigning or use your pictures of God's people and the planet from the Bible exercise 'To let?'

HELPFUL HINT

A NOTE ON CAMPAIGNING

Campaigning is an important feature of this resource. The ideas suggested in response to each session are a good place to start, but a campaign generally has more impact when a large number of people do the same action. If possible, try to keep up to date with the latest action for all the issues by visiting www.tearfund.org/campaigning.

Check out Tearfund's *Whose Earth?* campaign for the latest climate change actions!

THE DIFFERENT ISSUES...
WATER AND SANITATION

Without adequate management of water resources and access to water and sanitation, poverty eradication will never happen. Water and sanitation is intrinsically linked to such issues as health, nutrition, education, livelihoods, the role of women and the environment. Lack of access to water and sanitation primarily affects the poorest of the poor, especially women. Imagine having to wait all day to go to the toilet and then having to walk to a field in the dark, fearful of attack. This is the daily nightmare that many women in poor countries face because they don't have a toilet in their homes and their culture makes using public facilities difficult. Imagine having to watch your child eating faeces or play in sewage simply because they don't know any better, because they don't have a choice. Put simply, basic sanitation is about people having access to some kind of facilities that hygienically keeps human excreta separate from contact with other humans, animal or insects. We're not talking about en suite facilities with dual flush toilets, but sewers, septic tanks, pour-flush latrines or even simple pits latrines, provided that they are not public.[37] It's the kind of thing most of us take for granted. We probably don't think about where water comes from or where it goes, we just use it. If it weren't so readily available, perhaps we'd think about water differently, perhaps our priorities would change.

Thousands of children are dying each day because they don't have access to clean water or aren't educated about proper sanitation. In rural Africa, basic hygiene such as washing hands is often neglected because people don't understand the links between hygiene and disease, and their water is so precious that it's more of a priority to use it to drink and cook. Women often have to collect water from rivers, lakes, a well, a pump or a communal tap. Can you imagine walking seven miles every day just to get enough to drink and cook? It is not only physically difficult but it takes up a vast amount of time. Women are not able to do other important tasks and children are unable to go to school, as they are needed to carry out household chores. Lack of access to safe water and basic sanitation traps many of the world's poorest people in poverty, and may prevent many of the Millennium Development Goals (MDGs) from being met.[38]

The United Nations (UN) recognizes the fundamental place of clean water in poverty reduction. The MDGs aim to halve world poverty by reducing the proportion of people without access to safe water and sanitation by half, reducing child mortality by one-third and ensuring that all of the world's children gain access to primary education by 2015. To ensure the goals are met, the UN launched in 2005 'Water for Life 2005–2015', the International Decade for Action. UN Resolution 58/217 highlights how important water and sanitation are to achieving all of the goals, stating that: 'water is critical for sustainable development, including environmental integrity and the eradication of poverty and hunger, and is indispensable for human health and well-being.'[39]

FACE FACTS

● Four out of ten people around the globe do not have access to a simple pit latrine, and one-fifth have no source of safe drinking water.[40]

● Half of all hospital beds in the world are filled with people suffering from water-related diseases such as malaria, diarrhoea and trachoma, an eye disorder.[41]

● Each year 2.2 million people die from diseases directly related to drinking contaminated water. Diarrhoea alone claims the lives of nearly 6000 children a day.[42]

With more than 6000 children dying each day due to water-related diseases, and many millions more having to spend large parts of the day fetching and carrying water, the impact that reliable sources of clean water can have on attaining the MDGs is clear. Kofi Annan, United Nations Secretary General, says: 'We shall not finally defeat AIDS, tuberculosis, malaria, or any of the other infectious diseases that plague the developing world until we have also won the battle for safe drinking-water, sanitation and basic healthcare.'[43]

With a secure close supply of safe water and access to basic sanitation and the health benefits this brings, children have time to go to school, health costs are reduced, women have time to work and families can begin to help themselves out of poverty. Surely we have a responsibility to do whatever we can to make water and sanitation more available to more people.

SESSION 3
WATER AND SANITATION

Aim: To show how important water is for life, and to underline that some people don't have easy access to it. To think about how our attitudes could change towards water locally, nationally and globally.

You will need: An old 'page-a-day' diary, water bottles, OHP pens, Bibles, pens, paper, buckets, clean plastic containers, plastic cups, bin bags, *Resource 3A: Case study*, local map, drawing pins, a glass of dirty water, length of string frozen in a block of ice, tea lights, *Resource 3B: Drama*.

Thought shower (10 mins)

Hand out a sheet of paper, or better still a page from an old page-a-day diary, to each person in your group. Starting when they get up in the morning, ask each individual to record the ways they use water in a typical day. Feedback answers to the whole group and record them so everyone can see them.

Ask the group to discuss their daily water usage and try to estimate how much water each activity requires.

FACE FACTS

- Bathing: On average each shower you take will use approximately 30 litres of water, compared to 110 litres in an average-sized bath. Some power showers can use more water than a bath – anything from 15 to 60 litres per minute.

- Toilets: The toilet is one of the largest users of water in the home. Toilets plumbed before 1993 will probably have a cistern that uses 9.5 litres of water per flush compared with 7.5 litres on more recent models.

Source: www.stwater.co.uk

Ask the group to think about other ways in which we use water, other than for daily use, e.g. fun things such as swimming, serious things such as putting out fires, etc. The point is that we have so much water that we can use it without thinking, and we can even use it to play! Finally ask the group to think about:

- What are the qualities of water?

- And why is it so important?

Bring out from the above suggestions some of the most vital ones. Conclude that water is life-giving, the most important natural resource we have as human beings.

A message in a bottle (10 mins)

Water is everywhere in the Bible. Pick out some of the Bible references from below, give them to your group, and ask them to talk about the different roles of water in each of these occasions:

Water sustains: Gen. 1:20; Jn. 4:1–42

Water saves: Gen. 2:9–11; Ex. 2:1–10; Ex. 14:16–31

Water serves: Jn. 9:5–7; Jn. 13:1–17

Label three empty one-litre water bottles: 'Sustains', 'Saves' and 'Serves'. Ask each individual, or small group if you decided to divide up your main group, to decide which bottle best fits their verse and to drop their message into the appropriate bottle. Feedback the answers once everyone has finished. Make the point that water in the Bible equals life, therefore to deny it to anyone is nothing short of unjust.

• •

Water, water, everywhere? (20 mins)

Split your group into teams, line them up, and place a full bucket of water opposite each team at the other end of the room. Hand each team a plastic cup, an empty container (clear if possible), and one bin bag (to keep their clothes dry!). Each team has to transfer as much water as they can from the bucket opposite to their container using only the plastic cup. As they run in the form of a relay to fill their container, the cup has to be balanced on the heads of each team member – hence the protective bin bag. You might want to put in an obstacle or two to make it trickier.

• •

All around the world x 3 (10 mins)

Although the previous exercise may have been fun, for some people in the world, that's exactly how they get their water. They don't have taps bringing it to their homes, and so they have to get up early and walk for a very long time, maybe a couple of hours, so that they can bring water back to their homes. Consider the following case study (*Resource 3A: Case study*):

PEOPLE AND POVERTY
CASE STUDY – TANZANIA

Joyce Mbwilo lives in Uhambingeto in Tanzania. She is 30 years old and has four children. Until recently, Joyce used to have to walk 14 miles every day to fetch water for her and her family. Joyce has effectively walked three times around the world during her lifetime. Joyce explains: 'Before the water supply project started here, I used to get up right in the middle of the night, at midnight, take my bucket and go to fetch water. I was back at 10 a.m. the next day. The water was just 20 litres in a bucket. My family were very many, so 20 litres was not much, but this is the life I first lived, before this new project came.'

Thanks to a Tearfund-supported project, villagers have been able to locate a spring and install a system of pipes that now provide clean water for drinking, cooking and washing for Joyce's community.

Source: Tearfund

- What is your initial reaction to Joyce's story?

- Think about a place seven miles from you. How long would it take you to travel by car, bus or to walk?

Try and get hold of a local map and ask people to guess where seven miles would be (give them a coloured drawing pin to mark their estimate). How long would it take to walk that far? If you have time, hand out a bucket full of water and ask for volunteers to stand holding it with their arms stretched out in front of them. See who can do it the longest.

- How do you imagine it would feel to carry 20 litres (about the weight of two one-year-old children) for seven miles?

- What kind of things would you need to think about to keep you going? What do you imagine Joyce thought about to keep her going?

- What would you do if you spilt it?

If Joyce spilt her water, she wouldn't have enough for that day and so would have to walk all the way back and get more. That's how precious water is to her.

• •

Food and drink (5 mins)

Another problem for people living in poorer communities is that even if they can get water it might make them very sick, or even kill them. You could use the drama on the CD-ROM (*Resource 3B: Drama*) to help explain how in many parts of the world water is so scarce that people will use dirty water. They have to get it wherever they find it: a muddy river or lake, where people and animals swim, or where clothes are washed – extremely dirty places. Pass around a glass of very muddy horrible water and ask if anyone would like to taste it. (Don't let them!) Naturally, drinking this kind of stuff can lead to all kinds of illnesses.

> **FACE FACTS**
>
> Around 30,000 children have died today from preventable diseases, dirty water and poor sanitation.[44]

• •

Water matters (5 mins)

Why is it that some of us in the world are within seconds of access to water, while others have to walk miles to get it? Why is it that most of us are free to drink clean water at any point during the day, whilst others have to drink dirty water that makes them sick or could cost them their life? Sometimes, the people with power in the world, the people who make the decisions, don't always listen to the poor people, so it's up to us to stick up for the people who can't stick up for themselves, and speak out for the people whom no-one listens to (Prov. 31:8–9).

WATER – A DIFFERENT WAY . . .

Globally – called to serve

The *Water Matters* campaign initiated by Tearfund and WaterAid urged the UK government to ensure that water and sanitation issues were prioritized at the World Summit on Sustainable Development held in August 2002. Just before the Summit, Deputy Prime Minister John Prescott accepted more than 120,000 signatures to the Water Matters petition at No.10 Downing Street.

The *Water Matters* campaign was a success. Water and sanitation issues were prioritized. New targets and programmes of action were put in place for the world's poorest people, notably a target to halve the proportion of people without access to sanitation by 2015. This was a vital step in a process that will ultimately change the lives of millions. Now the challenge for the world community is to make sure that we see practical action. Keep praying:

- for people without water – that God would give them what they need and that he would help the people in their countries who are doing their best to change the situation

- for projects which help people to access water and basic sanitation, and provide education on the benefits of clean, safe water and basic sanitation

- for problems caused by floods or drought – that lives threatened or affected by the destruction of the environment would find comfort

- that leaders in poorer countries will start to listen to people who need their help

- that our Prime Minster would listen to our request to respond to problems people face with water

- that all governments would play their part in finding the resources to meet the MDG targets so that millions can get safe water and sanitation

- that Christians will take a lead in making decisions about their own lifestyle that will have a positive impact on people and planet.

If you'd like to be creative you could choose to fill one of your empty water bottles, perhaps the one labelled 'serves', with your prayers.

HELPFUL HINT

FAMILY SERVICE RESOURCE

Old Testament TV (OTTV) is a Tearfund CD-ROM designed to provide a unique and topical way of presenting the Bible through the eyes of on-the-spot television reporters. In *Thirsty*, Moses and the Israelites run out of food and water. Call 0845 355 8355 (ROI 0044 845 355 8355) to order your copy.

Locally – called to save

Using your water diary, try to think about where you could cut back on your use of water. Here are just a few ideas:

IN THE KITCHEN

● If you ever wash up or peel vegetables, use a bowl rather than the sink – you could pour the waste water onto the garden.

● Strain away any fats and food scraps from your dishwater and use the remaining water on your plants. It won't harm your plants. In fact, this type of water is excellent for getting rid of bugs.

● Always try to use the plug and don't let the tap run when you're washing your hands or washing up.

IN THE BATHROOM

● Take a shower instead of a bath – this can save more than 300 litres of water a week. Be careful though: a power shower can use more water than a bath![45]

● Turn off the tap when brushing your teeth – you could save eight litres per minute.[46]

● Try placing a cut-down plastic bottle filled with water, in your cistern. If the bottle holds half a litre of water, that's how much water you'll save with each flush (some local water authorities offer free Save-a-Flush devices to cut down on water – contact yours to see how to get one).

Make a start today: take your empty water bottle, labelled 'saves', cut it down, and place it in the loo cistern where you meet. Every time you flush, think about other areas in the home, at school, college or work where you could save water. Encourage individuals in your group to chat to their parents or guardians about reasons why they might like to do the same once they get home!

HELPFUL HINT

BUT HOW DOES THIS IMPACT OTHERS?

Saving or monitoring your use of water will not directly impact people living in the many poorer communities around the world who lack access to clean, safe water and basic sanitation. What it will do is help you realize how much you do take it for granted and hopefully as a result begin to motivate you to take action for the sake of others who can't. At the very least, saving water will save the person paying the bill money; money that reinvested wisely could save someone else's life.

Nationally – called to sustain

We need to continue to put pressure on the UK government to provide more and better funding to improve water and sanitation for the world's poorest people. Look again at your page-a-day diary from the start of the session. Talk about the ways we use water, how we take it for granted and what changes you are prepared to make. Everyone deserves to be able to choose to use water as we do. Why not send your water diary off to your local MP and ask them to raise this issue with the current Secretary of State for International Development? You could send your letters in your final water bottle, the one labelled 'sustains'.

HELPFUL HINT

Remember to check out Tearfund's Whose Earth? campaign for the latest campaign actions on water and sanitation. Co-ordinated action = greater impact! Visit www.tearfund.org/campaigning.

THE DIFFERENT ISSUES...
CONFLICT

Poverty and conflict are often linked – which comes first is a little bit of a 'chicken and egg' situation. Poverty is often an influential factor in conflict and the buying of arms. In turn, conflict is also a root cause of poverty, important in itself, but also intertwined with other causes.

Disruption: Wars naturally hit food production badly. Civilian jobs may be cut and family breadwinners may go away to fight – some will be killed or injured, leaving the ongoing problem of caring for widows, orphans and disabled people. Transport (to market, for example) may be disrupted or rendered too dangerous. Food imports may also be cut back, to pay for arms imports. Exports may be hindered, especially if there is an external trade embargo.

Displacement: Displaced people put a serious strain on resources in the area to which they flee. They cease to be self-sufficient because they cannot plant crops for themselves, and so become dependent on relief supplies. In recent years there have been conflict-related famines in Ethiopia, Mozambique, Chad, The Sudan, Liberia and Somalia.

Destruction: Agricultural land, vegetation, water sources and seas may be destroyed or polluted as a result of conflict. Even if they are not completely destroyed, access to them may be denied by unexploded ordnance, or by the laying of mines – and these may remain a threat for years. The warring parties may well deliberately target vital infrastructure. In Mozambique's civil war, about 68 percent of the primary school network and one-third of all rural health units were destroyed or closed down.[47] Road, rail and oil-pipeline links that are vital to the economic independence of southern Africa from South Africa were persistently disrupted.

Distortion of the economy: Inflation, currency devaluation, panic buying, hoarding and racketeering may become problems. The government may find it hard to collect tax revenue, putting further pressure on social spending.

Distribution of arms: The wide availability of arms is a big problem. It is estimated that there are around 639 million small arms and light weapons in the world today, with an incredible 8 million more being produced every year.[48] Many of these arms exist as part of an illicit arms trade, which places illegal weapons in the wrong hands and, as a result, increases the risk of violent conflict, state repression, crime, and domestic abuse. UN Secretary-General, Kofi Annan highlights how: '...the excessive accumulation and illicit trade of small arms is threatening international peace and security, dashing hopes for social and economic development, and jeopardizing prospects for democracy and human rights.'[49]

With quicker firing and more powerful weapons becoming more widely available, many people's lives are under greater threat. Even legal weapons, in particular guns, are easy to get hold of since the trade is largely unregulated. Unless governments begin to restrict the spread of arms the situation will only get worse, human rights violations will increase, and the amount of people able to escape poverty will decrease. The shocking reality is that many governments and companies largely ignore the fact that the flow of arms tends to head in the direction of those who openly disregard the laws of international human rights. If that wasn't bad enough it seems odd that those regarded as the world's peace keepers, i.e. the five permanent members of the UN Security Council: the USA, UK, France, Russia and China, seem to profit most from people's misery. They are responsible for 88 percent of reported conventional arms exports.

FACE FACTS

From 1998 to 2001, the USA, the UK, and France earned more income from arms sales to developing countries than they gave in aid.[50]

So what about you; how are you involved in conflict? Are you into pacifism or participation when it comes to dealing with tricky situations? Is a decision to go to war ever that black and white? Of course there may be ways you're already involved in conflict but you just don't know it. Read on.

SESSION 4
CONFLICT

Aim: To understand where, why and how conflict happens around the world. To find ways of recognizing what triggers war and the consequences. To explore ways of responding to conflict situations personally, locally, nationally and globally.

You will need: lots of old newspapers (ideally ones including local, national and global stories), masking tape, wet wipes, lining paper, pens, sticky notes, reusable sticky pads, Bibles, pens, *Resource 4A: Case study, Resource 4B: Printable, Resource 4C: Printable.*

One armed combat (20 mins)

Divide into four teams; nominate one person from each team to be the 'warrior'. Wrap the 'warrior' in newspaper from head to toe, leaving only their left arm and right eye uncovered. Have two 'warriors' competing against each other at one time, the aim being to try to rip as much newspaper off the other as they can. Divide the game into 'rounds', so when they're not fighting, teams can repair their warrior. Feedback as a group how the game felt.

• **Warriors:** How did it feel during combat?

• **Team mates:** What did it feel like to see your warrior winning or loosing?

• What different kinds of emotions did you go through as the battle went on?

A moving target? (10 mins)

Draw a circle (about the size of a hula hoop) in the centre of a huge sheet of wallpaper lining. Draw two other concentric circles around the first to form two outer zones (see diagram on page 33). Hang your newly created 'target' on a wall or place it over the floor and encourage your group to gather around. Read James 4:1– 3 together and then ask your group: What different kinds of factors seem to cause conflict in your life?

Encourage your group to discuss their causes of conflict and then to write their feelings in the centre circle using marker pens. After an appropriate amount of time, begin to move on to focus on some of the symptoms of conflict which are apparent locally, nationally and globally. Sift through the newspapers from the game and try to find remnants of stories of local, national and global conflict – stick these in the relevant zones to form a large conflict collage. Once the collage is complete encourage feedback. Ask:

● In one word, how would you describe your feelings about the conflict that exists around the world?

● In what ways are the symptoms of conflict linked to some of the same sorts of emotions that cause conflict for you?

● As you begin to see links between causes and symptoms, begin to draw in lines that connect the centre of your target to the outer zones. Use marker pens or string and sticky tape.

● If some symptoms don't seem to have core causes, add additional words to the centre of the target and draw in the links.

Make the point that although we may look at global conflict and wonder what it's got to do with us, some of the factors that trigger it aren't too dissimilar to the causes of conflict in our own lives. We really ought to be able to relate better to conflict in other people's lives because, we either have:

a similar feelings to the people who cause it

b some idea of what it feels like to experience its symptoms – or do we (see Charles' story below)?

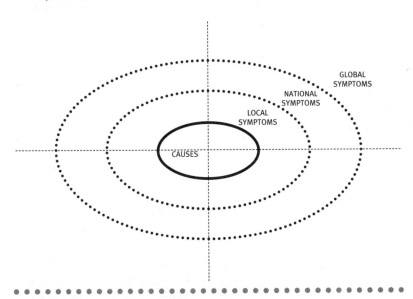

● ●

Combat consequences (5 mins)

Having briefly considered some of the possible causes and symptoms of conflict, pause to think through some of the consequences of war. Use the following case study (*Resource 4A: Case study*) to stimulate people's thinking and take feedback after they have had time to consider conflict consequences.

PEOPLE AND POVERTY

CASE STUDY – UGANDAN CHILD SOLDIERS

Charles' story begins seven years ago, when as an eight-year-old child visiting his grandmother he was abducted and forced to fight for the Lord's Resistance Army (LRA), Uganda's lawless rebels. Shot in his leg and lower back, he was forced to act against his will. He's uncertain how many people he killed but thinks it was three, '...two with a stick. One I shot with a gun,' he says.

Charles was regularly beaten, on one occasion 200 times for leaving a bomb behind. Listening to Charles' story it's hard even to begin to understand how his experiences must have affected him. The LRA rule their child soldiers by fear, forcing them to commit acts that will haunt them for years. Charles was no exception, as he explains: 'To stop me from escaping they abducted someone for me to kill. I had to kill that person using a stick. I just beat him to death with a stick.'

As shocking as Charles' story is, it's even more shocking to know that there are thousands more that may never be heard. Charles' experiences are not unique. It is estimated that 28,500 Ugandan children have been abducted since 1985, and while they may not have been forced to fight, their experiences with the LRA will leave scars that may never vanish.

Unholy war? (20 mins)

So what does God say about conflict, war and aggression? At first sight, the whole issue of war is a little confusing in the Bible, particularly in the Old Testament. In order to encourage your group to have an open debate on their view of war, split into two smaller groups: one should argue YES in favour of conflict and the other should argue NO against it. Use the Bible references (below) and the images and stories of conflict that you've already found in your newspapers as possible sources of background information for each group.

YES to war: Josh. 8:1; Num. 31:7; Deut. 3:22; Deut. 20:1–4

NO to war: Deut. 1:41–42; 1 Kgs. 12:24; 1 Chr. 22:8; Ps. 120:7; Mt. 5:17–26,38–48

Divide the time you have into small-group preparation (5 mins), group-to-group presentation (5 mins), and then finally a larger discussion (10 mins). At the end of the debate ask individuals to step out of their roles, summarize their own feelings towards war, and then vote: YES or NO. You could hold a secret ballot if you like.

Yeh but, no but, maybe? (10 mins)

Is considering conflict ever as simple as deciding between YES and NO? A decision to go, or not to go to war isn't always that simple (something most us know from recent history). Surely some things are worth fighting for? What happens if there is no other option? Is war ever justified? And if so, can it ever be 'just'? Christian ethicists have developed what they describe as criteria for just war (*Resource 4B: Printable*):

'JUST' WAR?

● War should only be fought for a just cause, such as in response to violent aggression (which may include aggression against a third party).

● The intention should be to restore a just peace.

● War should only be a last resort.

● The decision to go to war should only be made by a legitimate authority.

● There should be a reasonable hope of success.

Non-combatants should never be directly or deliberately attacked (under the principle of discrimination). The human, financial and environmental costs of military action should not outweigh the likely gains (the principle of proportion).

Source: *The Costly Game*, Tearfund

Feedback your feelings about whether a just war is ever possible, and, if you have time, discuss the appropriateness of the criteria above. Perhaps encourage your group to draw up their own criteria for or against a just war. As you move on to consider a different way to address conflict, you'll need to consider the implications of Jesus's model of pacifism (being a peacekeeper/conscientious objector), particularly where war seems inevitable. Jesus may be a 'pacifist' because he accepts personal injustice against himself, but what does the fact that he's very proactive when God's honour or the well-being of the weak are at stake make him?

CONFLICT — A DIFFERENT WAY . . .

Locally – adjusting your aims

The key to our own struggles with conflict is to recognize the triggers early and to take steps to deal with them before they lead us into potentially damaging situations. Encourage individuals to think through ways to combat the triggers before they lead to conflict. If it helps, read from Philippians 2:3–11, and then ask your group to think through what kind of attitude they need in order to combat those feelings that often lead towards conflict. Ask individuals or groups to write down a number of positive statements which they will aim to achieve in order to begin to conquer their conflict triggers.

Returning to the groups in which they opened the session, encourage them to create a 'missile' out of masking tape, newspaper, or even a couple of rolled up socks. Ask for a couple of volunteers to hold up the paper target you made earlier. Ask each group to throw their 'missiles' at the target, specifically aiming at the 'bull', to illustrate their intentions to combat those initial feelings that can often lead to anger, hate and suffering for themselves and for others.

Make the point that with positive action it is possible to combat conflict early. With those feelings that lead to anger removed, the links to conflict no longer exist – literally!

HELPFUL HINT

You may want to leave your group with a simple tip on dealing with conflict in their own lives. Ephesians 4:26 says, 'Do not let the sun go down while you are still angry.' That means if you have a problem with someone, sort it out. Don't go to bed and let it get worse: deal with it.

You may feel it's appropriate to finish by allowing some time for your group to reflect on any outstanding issues of conflict that they need to sort out.

Nationally – anger management?

The thought of positively affecting other people's experiences of conflict, particularly those overseas, may leave you completely stumped – what good can you realistically do? You may find the verse from Ephesians 4 (above) a real challenge for yourself, but what if you took it a step further: it could mean that if you see problems beyond your own situation which make you angry, then don't rest until you've taken whatever steps you can to bring about positive change. All conflict is not bad, some is necessary if we're ever to bring justice to unjust situations. You may have already discussed during the session whether war can ever be just, but focus for a minute on whether *anger* can ever be just. In John 2:14–16 Jesus demonstrates what has become known as 'righteous anger'. Something he sees upsets him so much that he is driven to conflict for the sake of justice.

Discuss in what ways Jesus's anger is appropriate/inappropriate in this situation. Ask:

- Why do you think he got so angry?

- Are there situations in your world that make you equally angry?

- In what ways do you feel your anger is justified?

BIBLICAL BACKGROUND

Although the word 'righteous' is not present in the text here in John, this is the label that has been attached to Jesus's actions on this occasion in his life and ministry. In both Hebrew and Greek there is no distinction between 'righteousness' and 'justice'. They are both about hungering for a right relationship with God, which means striving for what is right and just for others and for the earth and its creatures.

Believe it or not there are people around the world who are making money out of conflict. If we follow the example of Jesus it would seem that we are well within our rights to express a degree of anger at this injustice if we see fit. Some of those people making money could be from your country!

- Are you sure your bank, or the place you plan to bank, doesn't invest in arms? How would you feel if they did?
- Are you aware of how involved your government is in the arms trade?
- In what ways do you feel the arms trade has a negative or positive effect on our national life and the lives of others?
- What is its policy on selling arms? Is it just?
- Is the argument, 'if we do not supply arms, others will', really a just argument?
- If your government is subsidizing arms exports, should it?
- Is it possible to control the final use/misuse of weapons?
- Are their better ways in which our government could influence areas of conflict and potential conflict across the world?

A world without arms would be a far better place, but in a very imperfect world we may have to face up to the fact that trade in this lucrative area is inevitable. Perhaps the challenge for us is how we hold people to account and ensure the arms trade is as just as it ever can be. An agreement on arms that ensures all governments adhere to the same basic international standards would be a good start. The success of the international campaigns to ban landmines proves that many governments do take notice of public opinion. Perhaps you've never thought about how arms could ever be just; the following thoughts may help you as you begin to form your own ideas about how best to respond (*Resource 4C: Printable*). Visit www.controlarms.org for information about ways to campaign.

PEOPLE AND POVERTY

'JUST' ARMS?

A just arms trade will take account of a country's other needs (health, education, development, and so on).

- Arms should not be sold to those engaged in aggression or human rights abuse.
- Arms should not be sold where they will create tension, and make war more likely.
- Arms should only be sold to countries already at war if they have exhausted all other possibilities, are intent on creating a just peace, and have a reasonable hope of success.
- Arms should only be sold to legitimate authorities (this might include rebel forces with widespread popular support).
- Arms should not be sold where there is a possibility of their being deliberately used against civilians, or where the weapons are indiscriminate (e.g. landmines).

Source: *The Costly Game*, Tearfund

Globally – a safe place

Uganda prides itself on being an African success story. Uganda prefers to tell people about debt relief, HIV and AIDS prevention, and exotic tourism rather than reveal the truth about the war in northern Uganda that is nearly two decades old.

PEOPLE AND POVERTY

NIGHT COMMUTERS

Jackline, like 95 percent of the population of Acholiland (the region most affected by conflict in Uganda), lives in a camp created by the government. They are supposed to be 'safe zones', but attacks on camps by the Lord's Resistance Army (LRA) are common and often fatal. People are so afraid of the LRA that every night approximately 45,000 women and children leave their homes and head for the relative safety of nearby towns. These night commuters face a walk of up to six miles to find a bit of floor space in the grounds of the hospital, the lorry park or, failing that, on the streets.

Jackline is six-months pregnant but brings her two young children with her every night. 'The children struggle with the walk. They are too small for such distances,' she says. 'When it rains we don't have shelter. It just rains on us. We can't sleep so we stand until it stops. But I am trying to run away from the LRA and I feel safer when I am here because there are many people around us.'

Source: *activist 39*, Tearfund

Noah's Ark, a Tearfund partner, offers safety and security for many of the people caught up in the conflict in Uganda. Its centre offers people the chance to play volleyball or football or do homework before sleeping in safety. Whilst some accuse the government for allowing the violence to continue, others blame the international community for failing to step in. Whatever the answer to Uganda's problems, it is clear that work such as that of Noah's Ark is vital if thousands like Charles and Jackline are to pick up the pieces of their lives once again.

● Pray for development organizations and individuals involved in areas of conflict around our globe.

● Perhaps you could contact them to find out how you could help.

THE DIFFERENT ISSUES...
ASYLUM

The term 'asylum seeker' is used to describe someone who is seeking refuge in a particular country due to conflict, persecution or disaster. As a refugee from another country they are usually granted food and shelter by their host nation and protected by international laws whilst a decision is made as to whether they may be granted asylum, i.e. the right to stay, or enabled to return home. Someone fleeing their home but remaining in their own state is known as an Internally Displaced Person (IDP). Unlike refugees, they are likely to be trapped in whatever situation caused them to flee in the first place. Often seen as 'enemies of the state,' they are not protected by the same laws as refugees and therefore their fate is often at the mercy of their own government. Despite millions of people in countries such as Afghanistan, Angola, Bosnia and Sri Lanka returning home in recent years, the estimated number of IDPs is around 25 million, since similar numbers are currently being displaced in areas like Colombia, Burundi, Africa's Congo basin and the Sudan.[51]

Asylum seekers in our country are some of the most marginalized and vulnerable people in the UK, often living in poor accommodation and with limited access to services. Many refugees arrive in the UK having fled conflict zones and human rights abuse and endured gruesome journeys. On arrival they may then be taken to accommodation centres for months on end to wait for news on their application. In many communities they are viewed with hostility, suspicion and prejudice. Young people are no more liberal than older generations on the issue of asylum seekers:

FACE FACTS

In a MORI poll:

- 58 percent of 15–24 year olds felt that asylum seekers make 'no positive contribution to this country'.

- Only 51 percent of interviewees believed that asylum seekers deserved equal human rights to British citizens.

- 48 percent agreed that 'few asylum seekers are genuine'.

- 56 percent believed that the United Kingdom should offer a safe haven to 'genuine' cases.

Source: MORI poll for National Refugee Week, 2003

There are many myths surrounding asylum seekers:

- **They're attracted by the UK's generous benefit system** – Asylum seekers aren't allowed to claim mainstream welfare benefits. If they are destitute, their only option is to apply for support with the National Asylum Support Service (NASS); they receive about £39 per week, 30 percent below the poverty line. Asylum seekers are prohibited from working until they are given a positive decision on their asylum case, and these decisions can take years. Such conditions are unlikely to entice them to leave their homes and endure difficult journeys to live here.

- **We take more than our fair share of refugees** – At the end of 2003, the UK hosted 79,000 refugees, which is equivalent to only 0.1 percent of the population.[52] The UK ranks ninth among EU countries in terms of asylum applications received. It is the poorer nations that absorb the bulk of refugees, even though they lack the resources to look after them.

- **Only a handful of asylum seekers are genuine** – An estimated 28 percent of applications result in grants of asylum, temporary status, or allowed appeals. Once granted asylum a person is a refugee.[53] The terms 'illegal refugee' and 'illegal asylum seeker' are misnomers. While some asylum seekers use illegal means to enter the UK, they may still have a genuine case for claiming to be a refugee. Article 31 of the Convention Relating to Refugees (1951) says that governments cannot penalize refugees who have to use false documents to enter a safe country.

- **Refugees are a burden on the UK taxpayer, and swamp our public services** – Research suggests that migrants add to the wealth of receiving countries. They rely less on welfare services than local populations; they are usually young, want to work hard, and create as many jobs as they occupy.

- **They are uneducated and unskilled** – The *New Internationalist* reported in October 2002 that 33 percent of asylum seekers have a degree or professional qualification, compared with 15 percent of the British population; 65 percent speak two languages; 66 percent had jobs in their own countries.[54]

So what are your views on asylum seekers and global refugees? Are they any different from those above?

SESSION 5
ASYLUM

Aim: To raise awareness of the plight of asylum seekers and refugees and to explore ways of serving them in our communities.

You will need: Masking tape or rope, music, *Resource 5A: Worksheet*, pens, paper, *Resource 5B: Printable*, flameproof container, matches, *Resource 5C: Case study*, Bibles, internet access, world map, drawing pins, coloured wool or string, *Resource 5D: Case studies*, Blu-tack.

Just arrived (as people arrive)

Split your venue in two using some form of tape or rope. Label each half with two different random words (ideally using letters from a foreign alphabet), e.g:

<table>
<tr><td>σηεεπ</td><td>γοατσ</td></tr>
</table>

Try to get hold of a piece of loud, unusual, foreign or even distorted piece of music and play this as loud as possible as people arrive. Hand out 'Welcome sheets' to each individual (*Resource 5A: Worksheet*), and ask people to complete them. (They won't know where to start as they're in a foreign language.) Separate individuals and make them sit on either side of the line. If you have any linguists in your team select a few individuals and begin to interrogate them in a foreign language. At a suitable point, stop the music and explain that this is what it's like to be in an 'alien' environment, to be a stranger in a strange land.

HELPFUL HINT

The above exercise could be distressing for some, particularly if they have experienced something similar themselves. If you have any doubts, don't do it or adapt it to suit the make-up of your group.

Get packing (10 mins)

Split your group into smaller groups and ask them to discuss the following with each other: five things you wouldn't want to leave behind if you had to leave your home in the next five minutes.

Explain that we all probably assumed that packing meant knowing where we were going, or going on holiday. But this can be a real dilemma for many people around the world. Fighting or terror may have come close to their homes and they have had to run for their life. They may well have to run or walk, so they can only take what they can carry. When people like this cross a border into another country, they are called refugees. They are not known as asylum seekers until they begin to apply to stay in the country to which they have fled to find safety.

Wish we weren't there (20 mins)

This activity will give your group an initial insight into what it may feel like to be a refugee. Hand out a sheet of A4 paper to each person. (Alternatively use the postcard template – *Resource 5B: Printable*. Print the sheets back to back to resemble a post card.)

Take feedback after each stage, but pretend not to pay much attention or show any real interest.

On the front ask each individual to:

HOME	COMMUNITY
Draw a quick sketch of where they live	Draw a quick map of their community, including local landmarks and marking on places: ● where you feel safe ● where you don't feel safe ● which are the best areas to live ● which are the worst areas to live ● where you spend most of your time

On the back ask each individual to:

AMBITIONS	RELATIONSHIPS
List their top ten hopes and dreams	Make a list of their family members (in order of preference if you like)

> **HELPFUL HINT**
>
> Do be sensitive, as similar things may have happened to young people in your group e.g. divorce, being kicked out of home.

Take the group, a flameproof container and a box of matches outside. Spend a couple of minutes in silence remembering everything that's been written, drawn, talked about and circled. Then set the whole lot of papers on fire. (Alternatively simply rip their papers up and drop them into a bin.)

Explain that what they have experienced reflects in some small way the experience of refugees all over the world. Their experience is like the match that burnt the papers: it consumes people's hopes, homes, families and countries.

● ●

Who and how? (5 mins)

The United Nations High Commission for Refugees' (UNHCR) definition of a refugee is anybody who 'has left his or her own country or is unable to return to it owing to a well-founded fear of persecution for reasons of race, nationality, membership of a particular social group or political opinion'. Ask your group to list as many ways as possible of what they think would cause people to become refugees.

> **HELPFUL HINT**
>
> Answers may include: war and ethnic conflict, human rights abuses, environmental problems, and urbanization.

Now ask your group to list what they think happens to these refugees.

> **HELPFUL HINT**
>
> Answers may include: immediate asylum, short-term settlement, return to their own country.

● ●

What's an asylum seeker? (5 mins)

In the Universal declaration of Human Rights adopted by the UN in 1948, Article 14 states, 'Everyone has the right to seek and enjoy in other countries asylum from persecution.' To be accepted as a refugee in the UK, you must first apply for asylum (literally 'shelter'). This can be done at the place you enter the UK ('port entry') or, for those who come as students, visitors or with false papers, later at the Home Office ('in country'). Each case is considered and one of three things happens:

1 You get refugee status and can stay in the UK.

2 You get Exceptional Leave to Remain (ELR) and can stay for four years, and then your case is reviewed.

3 You are refused and sent to another country.

The United Nations Convention of 1951 goes on to say that a refugee is a person who 'is outside the country of his/her nationality and is unable or, owing to such fear, is unwilling to avail him/herself of the protection of their country; or who, not having a nationality and being outside the country of his/her former habitual residence as a result of such events, is unable or, owing to such a fear, is unwilling to return to it'. Consider the following case study (*Resource 5C: Case study*).

PEOPLE AND POVERTY

CASE STUDY – BURUNDI

Sada's not sure how she originally arrived in the UK. She thinks maybe the Red Cross airlifted her out of the war in Burundi. When she tried to claim benefits, officials didn't recognize her from her photo. Taken as an asylum seeker, she was so disfigured by sickness and hunger, she looked a lot older than 25. Today her life is very different, her situation has improved, and she has moved on quite considerably. She is fluent in English, has gained computer skills, has gained additional qualifications, and is now training to be a nurse. She is now in a position to make a contribution to UK society.

Awkward benefit officers are nothing compared to the treatment some asylum seekers get in the UK. Newspapers and TV programmes sometimes brand asylum seekers with words such as 'scroungers', 'fakes', 'thieves' and 'cheats'. What's more, if you believe the papers, there's a tidal wave of illegal immigrants flocking to 'soft-touch' Britain. Some sections of the media suggest that asylum seekers expect to live in the lap of luxury at British citizens' expense. Is the UK an easy country for foreigners to enter and stay in?

Source: Tearfund

The issue of asylum seekers is a complex one. It's not just about what the papers and politicians say. It's true that not all asylum seekers are genuine: there are those who cheat the system. But there are also people who desperately need to escape their circumstances. The challenge for the UK as a country is to identify and support those in genuine need. The challenge for Christians is to look at the reality and look at the Bible. How should we treat people who are asylum seekers, people who come knocking on our door as strangers?

The word on the street (20 mins)

The New Testament teaching of Jesus is very clear about what our attitude ought to be towards others, namely: treat others as you want to be treated yourself (Mt. 22:34–40). That said, it's not always easy to do this, particularly when you feel that these 'others' are unfamiliar to us, and from what we regard as an 'alien' culture. The good news is that it's not a new problem. What can we learn from God's guidance in the Old Testament?

Using wallpaper lining, create a kind of filmstrip, using the following three frames to represent different phases in their experiences: past, present and future. Jot down some of your thoughts on how Israel dealt with strangers during their history by using some of the following Bible references.

Frame 1: Remember in the **past** when you were strangers

The so called 'aliens' mentioned in the Old Testament refers to people who were fairly settled, certainly not just passing through or waiting for the first opportunity to return home. The Hebrew word *gêr* refers to someone who stays among a strange people as opposed to a foreigner who moves on fairly quickly. These people had latched on to someone/a place in Israel for their protection/preservation. Key verses to look at here include:

Gen. 15:13; Deut. 23:7; 24:22

Frame 2: Remember in the **present** to learn from your own experience

The fact that Israel themselves had been strangers in Egypt ought to influence their attitude towards strangers in their midst once settled in the Promised Land. Reference to Solomon's census in 2 Chr. 2:17 proves that there was a considerable number of them: 153,600! Key verses to look at here include:

Ex. 22:21, 23:9; Deut. 23:7; Lev. 19:34

BIBLICAL BACKGROUND

It may be unclear why the 'aliens' were in Israel in the first place. They may have been remnants of people Israel had displaced, people drawn to Israel's God, economic migrants or those seeking refuge from danger elsewhere. The command however is quite clear: they were to be treated exactly like any fellow Israelite, i.e. the laws relating to just dealings between Israelites also applied to the aliens. In fact, they were put into the same category as the widows and orphans of Israel.

Frame 3: Remember in the **future** to treat others as you wish you were treated

The following verses suggest that strangers are not to be oppressed:

Ex. 22:21–22; Ps. 146:9; Jer. 7:6-7; Zech. 7:10; Ps. 94:6; Ezek. 22:7,29; Mal. 3:5; Lev. 19:33–34

Leviticus 19:34 is clear that the Israelites were commanded to love aliens as themselves. The following verses suggest that the strangers are to be loved:

Lev. 19:34b; Deut. 10:19

BIBLICAL BACKGROUND

What's important here is the reason given for loving the aliens: because the Israelites were once in the same position themselves. They had gone down to Egypt as welcomed guests, but in due course the Egyptians had turned against them and treated them very badly. God encourages them to remember the bitterness of that experience so that they would not inflict such bitterness on anyone else.

For most of us it's hard to imagine what it must be like to be a helpless stranger in an alien environment. It may be a good idea to do some imaginative role-play at this point. Think about:

● What situations you've faced in the past that have made you feel isolated, excluded and marginalized

● In what situations do you currently feel like a stranger in a foreign land?

● What kind of things would need to happen to quash these feelings?

● In what ways does the biblical experience of the aliens in Israel relate to twenty-first-century asylum seekers?

● In what ways do your experiences of needing 'shelter' relate to asylum seekers?

Justice for genuine asylum seekers could mean applications are easier to make and more quickly answered. Fair employment could mean people are given the opportunity to have jobs, rather than having to rely on benefits. Charity could mean they're treated more generously and allowed to be part of the community rather than isolated from it.

ASYLUM – A DIFFERENT WAY . . .

Globally – search (5 mins)

Including people is a part of being a Christian, and looking after strangers is a big deal in the Bible. Find out more about some of the countries and types of situations that asylum seekers come from. Use this to inform your attitude and how you choose to pray about the issues. A good place to start would be: www.refugeecouncil.org.uk/infocentre/index.htm.

● You could get hold of a world map and plot the places people seek asylum from.

● What kind of things are causing them to flee their country?

● Mark with a pin and a piece of string the journeys they will have made. Think about the impact of these kinds of journeys, emotionally as well as physically.

HELPFUL HINT

Enabling Christians in Serving Refugees (ECSR) is a network of Christians across the UK who are working on either a voluntary or professional basis with asylum seekers and refugees. The network enables groups to link up with each other to share learning and receive support, while also being able to access appropriate Christian resources. Tearfund has been very involved in developing ECSR. Their website will be well worth a visit if you feel called to take further action: www.ecsr.org.uk.

Nationally – support (10 mins)

Refugees and asylum seekers are spread right across the UK, giving Christians a real opportunity to demonstrate God's love in a practical way. Organizations such as Tearfund support several UK partners offering friendship and support. Many of the refugees come from countries where Tearfund has overseas partners, so these projects are a logical extension of its ministry. Display and consider the case studies below (*Resource 5D: Case studies*) and as a group ask yourself:

- How you feel about each example: Excited? Incapable? Hopeful?

- What, if anything, can you learn about how to respond to asylum seekers from each case study?

CASE STUDY – ST ROLLOX CHURCH, SCOTLAND

This church project, based in Sighthill, Glasgow, provides support and advice to 50–60 families seeking asylum. The church also has good links with other community groups doing similar work. Among the activities St Rollox offers are a clothing store, a parent-and-toddler group, an English class, a holiday club and a computer class. Individual families are given practical and spiritual support where needed. Christine Murray runs the scheme, which Tearfund supports.

'We're building bridges,' she explains. 'One of the main aims is integration. Local people and asylum seekers all come in.'

Jamalya, like many immigrants in Sighthill, has found hope through the St Rollox church asylum project. Whilst living in Asia, one act of kindness by her husband, Sujan, cost their family their home, their livelihood – and very nearly their lives. Trouble began when Sujan, a Christian, gave a Muslim colleague a lift home. Spotted by other Muslims who resented their interfaith friendship, he was arrested and beaten. Harassment, violence and death threats followed until the family was forced out of Asia. Three years later, life as asylum seekers in Sighthill, Glasgow, has proved just as tough, explains Sujan's wife Jamalya: 'The first day we came, some people shouted out of their car, "You ******* asylum seekers" and threw things at us. After one year some guys beat my husband very badly.'

Sujan's family is receiving assistance in lodging an appeal after their asylum application was denied. The courts doubted Sujan's story on the grounds that his country has no overt discrimination policy.

(The names have been changed to protect the individuals' identities.)

CASE STUDY – ILFORD HIGH ROAD BAPTIST CHURCH WELCOME CENTRE

Ilford Road Baptist Church in London cares passionately about socially isolated people within the community. Their Welcome Project offers a drop-in facility for refugees, a place where they can make friends and get advice. The Welcome Centre opens two days a week to provide a number of essential services including: hot meals, nurse led clinics, advice sessions, laundry services, shower facilities and friendship.

CASE STUDY – CITY LIFE EDUCATION AND ACTION FOR REFUGEES (CLEAR)

CLEAR is helping refugees in Southampton through a number of activities, such as an advice centre, English classes and a volunteer network. Recognizing how difficult it can be for refugees to find employment, CLEAR is helping individuals to overcome language and culture barriers and to develop skills such as literacy and numeracy. A new programme is also being developed to help small groups of refugees set up their own businesses.

CASE STUDY – THE WELCOME CENTRE

Penge, near Bromley in Kent, has seen an influx of refugee families over recent years. Action in Communities' Welcome Centre offers services such as an advice centre, education and training (such as English and literacy courses), and social activities. Refugee families and individuals are being helped from countries such as the former Yugoslavia, the Sudan, Iraq, Iran, Kurdistan, the Democratic Republic of Congo (formerly Zaire), Angola, Colombia and Somalia.

HELPFUL HINT

Visit the Enabling Christians in Serving Refugees (ECSR) website at www.ecsr.org.uk/local.htm for more information about how other local organizations are serving asylum seekers across the UK.

Locally – serve

It could be that your group is already, or will soon be, just down the road from people who are asylum seekers and refugees. What will you do? Call them scroungers, cheats and thieves, fearfully closing your doors to them – or maybe welcome them in, offering kindness, justice, help with work, charity and hospitality? It's your choice.

● Think of your own 'strange lands' – places where you feel uncomfortable.

● In these situations, what kind of things make you feel more at home?

● Are there things you could do to make others feel more welcome in your community?

● Produce a mind map of ideas that you could put into action as a group to welcome people to your community. (You may like to use the case studies opposite as a starting point.)

HELPFUL HINT

Things to think about might include: English classes, lunches, parties, holiday clubs, football clubs, games evenings, home visiting, making a local info pack, outings, food parcels, welcome packs, clothes, etc.

If there are asylum seekers at your school/college/university, maybe even in your class, why not make a point of being friendly to them? They may be shy at first, but keep trying!

No refugees locally? You can still get involved, maybe by offering holidays or donating money or furniture to projects.

For more ideas on how to respond to asylum seekers in your area, get hold of a free copy of Tearfund's Asylum Seeker and Refugee Befriending Pack. It includes loads of ideas about how to make a positive difference, plus the low-down on issues faced by refugees in the UK. Call 0845 355 8355 (ROI: 00 44 845 355 8355) or e-mail enquiry@tearfund.org to order your free copy.

THE DIFFERENT ISSUES...
HIV AND AIDS

HIV and AIDS is the leading cause of death in the majority world. It devastates families, communities, economies, social structures and leaves in its wake millions of orphans. Ninety-nine percent of all people suffering with AIDS-related illnesses live in the world's poorest countries.[55] Poverty in general makes people more vulnerable to infection; gender disparities, lack of access to healthcare and education further magnify the problem. HIV and AIDS is both a cause and an effect of poverty, as it affects the productive age group in society, thereby depreciating incomes while simultaneously increasing costs in order to provide health and social care for the sick.

Affected families are often forced to sell off assets and use savings to survive. They often need to pull children out of school so that they can help in the home or earn money. Family structures break down as a generation of parents die. The stigma related to HIV and AIDS exacerbates the fight against the pandemic. People with HIV are often denied access to healthcare, housing or employment, and can be shunned by family, friends and colleagues. Fear of discrimination prevents people from undergoing tests for HIV, seeking treatment, or acknowledging their status publicly. These are major obstacles to prevention and care. New anti-retroviral drugs are too expensive for poor people to buy. Treatment regimes can be complex, especially in environments where the health facilities are already depleted. Mortality rates are up to 20 times higher in countries that are poorer, and therefore people have less access to Anti-Retroviral Treatments (ARTs).[56] Although there is an increasing access to ARTs in some countries, the majority of people living with HIV do not have the choice to undertake treatment owing to high costs and limited access. The World Health Organization states that: 'Rolling out effective HIV and AIDS treatment is the single activity that can most effectively energize and accelerate the uptake and impact of prevention.'[57]

> **FACE FACTS**
>
> ● There are currently more than 40 million people living with HIV.[58] Fuelled by injected drug use, the epidemic is growing fastest in Eastern Europe and Central Asia.[59]
>
> ● 13.2 million children have been orphaned as a result of HIV and AIDS.[60]
>
> ● Only 8 percent of people living with HIV in developing countries have access to the HIV care and treatment they need – that's about 400,000 people. In the UK, we take treatment for granted, i.e. everyone is entitled to access.[61]

HIV and AIDS is a priority for development organizations like Tearfund. Tearfund supports a number of partners as they mobilize communities to respond to HIV and AIDS through prevention and care for people struggling with its impact. Partners address issues of vulnerability and the impact of HIV and AIDS among the poor. We can play our part too.

SESSION 6
HIV AND AIDS

Aim: To face up to some of the myths surrounding HIV and AIDS and as a result find a positive response to dealing with this devastating disease globally and perhaps locally.

You will need: Sticky notes, pens, *Resource 6A: Printable, Resource 6B: Worksheet, Resource 6C: Case study*, large paper, marker pens, Bibles, paper, paint, wet wipes, *Resource 6D: Case studies.*

So what do you know? (30 mins)

Part 1: Explain that during this session you'll be thinking about HIV and AIDS. Split your group into smaller groups and ask them to discuss what they know about HIV and AIDS. If you like, you could get your young people to write down their thoughts on stickies and stick them to the wall. At the end of the discussion time you could then separate their ideas into three columns:

● what you're sure is true

● what you're sure is false

● what you're sure that you don't really know.

HELPFUL HINT

The HIV virus is passed on from anything that allows infected body fluids to enter your bloodstream. You can get infected through unprotected sex, sharing a needle or syringe when injecting drugs with someone with the virus, using contaminated skin piercing equipment, or from an infected mother to her unborn child. You can also be infected through contaminated blood transfusions. You cannot get infected through mosquito bites, sharing a toilet seat, shaking hands, using the swimming pool or sharing knives and forks with an infected person. You often can't tell a person has HIV just by outward appearance. Only one in every ten people is aware that they are infected. The majority of poor people become ill with AIDS-related diseases within ten years; people with poor immunity develop AIDS-related symptoms much sooner. Although the gay community was the first to publicize the disease in the west, heterosexuals are just as vulnerable. There is no known cure for AIDS, but certain drugs can slow down the progression of the illness and delay the onset of AIDS.

Source: Tearfund and the Baptist Missionary Society.[62]

Part 2: Write out each of the letters from 'Human Immunodeficiency Virus' and 'Acquired Immune Deficiency Syndrome' on a piece of card or paper, and then cut out each individual letter (or use *Resource 6A: Printable*). If you choose to do this activity in small groups you should have 63 separate cards for each group (including spaces). Hand out a set of cards to each group and ask them to spell out the phrase to which each acronym relates.

HELPFUL HINT

HIV stands for Human Immunodeficiency Virus. The HIV virus infects the cells of the human immune system and begins to destroy or impair their function. It eventually leads to 'immune deficiency', at which point our body is no longer able to fight off infection and disease. Infection with HIV has been established as the underlying cause of AIDS.

AIDS stands for Acquired Immune Deficiency Syndrome. AIDS describes the collection of symptoms and infections, for example chest infections, digestive disorders, cancer and brain disease, which are associated with acquired deficiency of the immune system.[63]

See how each group does, take feedback on what each of them discussed as they were sorting their letters, and then use the following questions to help you discuss what HIV and AIDS actually is:

● Do you think the word *Immunodeficiency* in 'Human Immunodeficiency Virus' might give you any clues about what HIV actually is?

● What about the words 'Acquired Immune Deficiency Syndrome', what do you think AIDS is?

Every second counts (1 min)

Pair your young people off. Allow each pair just one minute to answer as many questions from *Resource 6B: Worksheet* as they can. The answers are: a) 1981; b) 3; c) 20; d) 14,000; e) 40, 60; f) 13; g) 99; h) 25; i) 1.6. At the end of the quiz, explain that every minute, five people die from AIDS. That means that during this game, five people will have died from AIDS-related illness. Ask five people to stand up in order to practically prove the point. HIV and AIDS is a global issue. Children are watching their parents die of AIDS. Where there are no grandparents or immediate family to look after them, children must set up home on their own.

Think about it (5 mins)

Unfortunately some Christians have not always had an easy time figuring out what they think about HIV and AIDS. Some lifestyles, such as homosexuality, sex work and drug taking, make people highly vulnerable to infection. Today the majority of people living with HIV are women, often married women, since according to UNAIDS: 'Women and girls often have limited access to essential education and healthcare services and often cannot choose to abstain from sex or insist on condom use. In addition, they are often coerced into unprotected sex, and are often infected by husbands in societies where it is common or accepted for men to have more than one partner.'[64]

HIV has a disastrous impact on the families – spouses, children and parents of the infected person. This makes the future very vulnerable for such families. Consider the following case study (*Resource 6C: Case study*):

PEOPLE AND POVERTY

CASE STUDY – CAMBODIA

Fifteen-year-old Sok Koun lives in Phnom Penh, Cambodia, in a ten-foot-square room that she shares with her brother, Arit, who's nineteen, and her two younger brothers. They've lost both of their parents to AIDS.

Their dad was sick for three months before he died. He'd been living in a rented room as traditional healers said their parents shouldn't be together because they were making each other worse. The landlord didn't let him stay there for very long because he was scared he might die, so eventually they had to take him to the countryside. Sok and Arit's mum became thinner, kept coughing and was sick for three or four years before dying in hospital. Sok and Arit's parents chose not to tell their children what they were dying of. The teenagers miss their parents. They used to talk together and both of them know their parents loved them very much.

An estimated 30,000 Cambodian children are orphaned by AIDS. The government provides no service for AIDS orphans. Thankfully Christians in Phnom Penh, are helping people like Sok and Arit through a Tearfund Partner called Project Halo (Hope, Assistance and Love for Orphans). Nayhouy Greenfield, one of Halo's founders, says: 'Some of the children we work with are under fifteen. Most of their life has been spent looking after a dying parent.'

Halo helps 250 children before and after a parent's death. They discuss plans for the future, make funeral arrangements, and care for grieving children. They also provide shelter, food, clothing and education.

Source: Tearfund

Draw three circles on a sheet of paper. As a group, consider the following three questions and write down your thoughts in each circle:

- Jot down words that describe how you feel about what you've just read.
- Jot down words which describe how you think Sok and Arit feel.
- Jot down words that describe how you think God feels.

Passing on compassion? (20 mins)

As we face up to our Christian responsibility to address HIV and AIDS, the focus should not be on how someone contracted the disease, but on how we show compassion to those who are suffering. HIV and AIDS has presented us with an opportunity to show tremendous love for people in great need. Check out these life-changing encounters Jesus had with individuals in need:

Matthew 8:1–3; 8:14–15; 9:20–22; 9:27–31; 14:34–36; 20:29–34.

Split into six groups and hand one passage to each group. Ask them to record the three most significant stages in each of Jesus's encounters with an individual in need. For example, in Matthew 8:1–3, Jesus touches, the person is willing, they are healed. Take feedback from each of the groups, asking people to comment in particular on the similarities and differences between each encounter.

BIBLICAL BACKGROUND

Sometimes Jesus approaches people, sometimes they approach him, but on each occasion in these examples of Jesus's life and ministry, he has to get alongside people for the healing to take place. Consider this:

A famous wildlife cameraman was once asked what the most difficult aspect of his job was. The interviewer, expecting to him to say travelling, irregular hours, mosquitoes or simply the dangerous situations he had to face to get the best shot, seemed slightly shocked when he replied, 'Helplessness.' To see a young cub lagging behind in danger of losing all contact with its father, falling behind as he treks through the jungle. To see a giraffe's newborn son struggling to get to its feet, her desperately nudging its lifeless body, knowing that if she doesn't, it risks losing it short life. To see a salmon losing its spirit and strength as it consistently fails in its attempts to jump up stream to lay its eggs. These are the things that make the life of even the most professional of observers tough. The constant tension between capturing the best shot whilst all the time holding back on an overwhelming desire to drop everything to step into the frame in order to make a difference to a life, was the hardest thing he faced as he viewed the wonder of God's creation from behind a camera lens.[65]

Contact = Compassion = Action. Through getting involved in the life of someone with HIV and AIDS it may not be possible to offer them healing from that particular disease, but their need often will be for recognition, acceptance, compassion or any number of other things which are entirely possible.

As Christians, the challenge facing us concerning HIV and AIDS is how to demonstrate the freedom that comes through trusting in Jesus as Saviour, to show that there is a God-way to live, but at the same time remembering that behind the numbers are husbands, wives, parents, children, farmers, teachers, doctors, politicians, bankers and business people. HIV and AIDS may seem like an impossible problem, but by finding a way to support people suffering its impact we're able to deal with the issue step by small step. All you have to do is get involved. All you have to do is be willing to touch the issue and the people affected by HIV and AIDS.

HIV AND AIDS – A DIFFERENT WAY...

Nationally – stop

AIDS can be treated. The epidemic can be stopped from spreading given the right drugs and better education. What is missing is the will of political leaders to act. The Stop AIDS Campaign brings together more than 80 of the UK's leading development and HIV and AIDS organizations. The campaign wants the UK government to be more committed to fighting HIV and AIDS internationally. The campaign also aims to see debt reduced so that vital resources can go into healthcare and education. The UK could lead the world in saving lives, by pushing for Access to Care and Treatment (ACT) for the 38 million HIV-positive people who need it. It would mean agreeing to:

● **Fund the fight**: $20 billion is needed by 2007.

● **Treat the people**: Lower the prices of life-saving AIDS drugs and other essential medicines.

● **Invest in health**: Enable poor countries to respond effectively to the AIDS crisis by improving the quality of their health services.

The Prime Minster will only do these things if enough people in the UK make it clear they see it as a priority. Write to your MP today and ask them to write to the Prime Minister, challenging him to make AIDS history. You can find the name of your MP at www.locata.co.uk/commons/ or call 020 7219 4272. Make sure you refer to ACT (see above) and don't forget to put your address and the date at the top. For more information about recommendations on how to make AIDS history, visit www.stopaidscampaign.org.uk.

If you want to be creative, why not send an HIV and AIDS 'fax sheet' to your MP. As a group, take a roll of fax paper, draw around your hands and try to fill one hand each with signatures. Include facts about HIV and AIDS and your thoughts about what the government ought to do.

Globally – look

Tearfund's partners recognize the link between poverty and vulnerability to HIV and AIDS. That's why their work is tackling the root causes of HIV and AIDS along with education, prevention and care. Through Tearfund partners' local experience and an ability to mobilize churches and other community groups, churches are playing a pivotal role in HIV and AIDS responses. Tearfund and other partner organizations are pressing for appropriate money, information and support to be made available to those working at community level. Look at the following case studies (*Resource 6D: Case studies*):

CASE STUDY – ZAMBIA

Through seminars, workshops and small group sessions, the Evangelical Fellowship of Zambia is raising awareness about HIV and AIDS among pastors and church leaders. The leaders are encouraged to mobilize their churches to care for orphans, children and families in their respective communities. Resulting activities include challenging congregations to show love to people with AIDS and encouraging local companies to teach affected families how to set up small businesses. Women from participating churches are trained in counselling and home-based care. To date, 110 orphans and vulnerable children's support initiatives have been started, with more than 73,000 children receiving spiritual care, counselling, education, clothes, blankets and food as a result of these initiatives.

CASE STUDY – BRAZIL

In Sao Paulo, Brazil, Tearfund partner Casa Filadelfia runs a drop-in centre for people affected by AIDS. The centre focuses on children, young people and their families, offering them emotional, spiritual and social support. At the centre, people can get healthcare advice, sexual health guidance, psychological support, careers guidance and legal advice. Casa Filadelfia also holds church services, runs Bible courses, and puts people in touch with local pastors and churches.

CASE STUDY – SIERRA LEONE

Young people (aged 15–24) account for nearly half of all new HIV infections worldwide. Tearfund partner Scripture Union Sierra Leone is working with young people aged 10 to 19 years in churches, schools and colleges, providing them with HIV and AIDS education and life-skills training. The focus of the project is on preventing young people from contracting HIV.

CASE STUDY – CAMBODIA

Tearfund partner Task is equipping communities in Cambodia to care for children who are living with or have been orphaned by HIV and AIDS. The project's youth mentoring scheme trains young members of local churches to link up with families affected by HIV and AIDS, to offer support and friendship.

CASE STUDY – INDIA

Tearfund partner the El Shaddai Resource Centre (ESRC) is providing care and rehabilitation to drug users and people with AIDS in Manipur State. Located on the Burmese border, Manipur is a corridor for the passage of drugs into India. The state has an estimated 40,000 drug users and 20,000 suspected HIV carriers. This project helps people get back into work by sponsoring training programmes. It also provides a clinic for people with HIV and AIDS and offers home-based care and education for people living with HIV and AIDS and their families. ESRC has also mobilized a number of community groups, such as a mothers' support group and a Bible study group, to offer support to addicts and people with AIDS in their communities.

In small groups, consider each of the case studies and pick out key themes and good practice. As a response, get your group to dip their hand in paint, make their mark on a piece of paper (or even better, on a large world map), and as they do so to pray about the different work that's going on with HIV/AIDS around the globe.

Another way you might like to support work in this area is by organizing a fundraising event or deciding as a group to give regularly. Send your gift to Tearfund, 100 Church Road, Teddington, Middlesex TW11 8QE. Alternatively call Supporter Enquiries on 0845 355 8355 (ROI 0044 845 355 8355) for more information.

• •

Locally – listen

HIV and AIDS is a global pandemic, which means it could just as easily be an issue in your local community as it is in your wider global community. Tearfund's partner, Grandma's, is a Christian charity aiming to give practical support to children and families affected by HIV, regardless of race, religion, gender, sexuality or lifestyle. For more information about Grandma's call 020 7610 3904. There may be similar organizations operating in your area that need support or volunteers. Perhaps local people may feel there is a need for one. Things you could offer as a group might include:

● babysitting, allowing parent(s) to go out

● taking a child out, enabling exhausted parents space for themselves, often just to sleep

● playing with children, giving them time and attention

● collecting a child from nursery or school and then spending time together

● taking time out and giving support to teenagers, allowing them the opportunity to be free of the role of carer for a few hours

● going with a family to hospital appointments, offering practical help and emotional support

● helping with group outings in the holidays.

Get the group to cut out the shapes of their hands on some coloured paper, and to write down some personal or group action points. Encourage them to place them in their Bibles (perhaps at one of the readings from Matthew they heard earlier), so that the next time they spend time listening to God they'll remember what they've promised.

HELPFUL HINT

EXPRESS COMMUNITY

 Express Community is a resource designed to enable small groups to better meet the needs of their local community. You may find some of the sessions and exercises it contains useful in discovering what the issues within your community really are. Published by Authentic Media, it is available from Tearfund, local Christian bookshops or www.wesleyowen.com priced at £7.99 (ISBN 1-85078-583-X).

THE DIFFERENT ISSUES...
TRADE

Global trade has the potential to lift millions of people out of poverty. Each minute, £5.5 million changes hands through the global trading system.[66] That's why trade is so important for poor countries in their fight against poverty. According to the Department for International Development (DFID), 'If Africa could increase its share of world trade by just 1 percent, it would generate five times more income than the continent currently receives in aid and debt relief.'[67]

However, the current unjust trading system, backed by governments of rich countries such as the UK, robs the poorest countries of £1.3 billion a day, which is 14 times more than they receive in aid.[68] Our current trading system works in favour of the rich and powerful. The more power a country has, the more it can push less powerful countries to trade on its terms rather than just ones. Rich countries are forcing the world's poorest countries to open up their markets to unfair trade in exchange for aid, loans or debt relief. Regions such as Europe contain many rich countries, which together can exert even more pressure on poor countries to open up their markets to EU goods. Europe is crafty too: it continues to subsidize its farmers heavily so that it can export European goods to poor countries where they will be cheaper than local farmers can produce them for.

Free trade for all is a myth. The notion of the global trading system being like a level playing field where every country gets the opportunity to play on an equal footing is completely unrealistic. The World Trade Organization (WTO) is the only global international organization set up to deal with the rules of trade between nations. However, it's often the rich countries, who demand that poor countries open up their markets to their goods in exchange for aid and trading opportunities, that hugely influence the WTO.

FACE FACTS

● International trade is worth $10 million a minute. Multinational corporations control 70 percent of this.[69]

● The average European cow receives $2.20 a day, whereas half the world's population of nearly three billion people struggle to survive on less than $2 a day.[70]

● If Africa, East Asia, South Asia and Latin America each increased their share of world exports by just one percent, they could lift 128 million people out of poverty.[71]

What's really needed is trade justice. As Christians, we need to fight for rules which ensure that governments, particularly in poor countries, can choose the best solutions to end poverty and protect the environment. We need the world's leaders to end export subsidies that damage the livelihoods of poor rural communities around the world and to make laws that stop big business profiting at the expense of people and the environment.

Of course, your shopping patterns have an impact on the rest of the world too. All you have to do is lift the label on your clothes to see that they have been made in some of the world's poorest countries. But have the companies who made them put their workers' rights first or have they exploited them in order to maximize their profits?

What about the food you buy: do you go for Fairtrade products or is your basket full of stories of how the people and the environment have been exploited to get the food to you? Let's commit to looking for the people behind our products, challenging companies and governments to put people before profit.

HELPFUL HINT

Find out how your lifestyle can speak up for the poor and how your money can benefit the poor at www.tearfund.org/liftthelabel.

SESSION 7
TRADE

Aim: To gain a basic understanding of the issues of world trade and how they affect the poor and to think about God's view on the situation.

You will need: One copy of *Resource 7A: Printable*, counters, sweets or pebbles, two variety packs of cereal (which usually include eight different mini boxes of cereal, costing about £1 per pack), one copy of *Resource 7B: Printable*, scissors, glue, Bibles, pens or pencils.

The molecule game (20 mins)

Divide your group into three, representing three tribes. Each tribe member is issued with a set of instructions (see *Resource 7A: Printable*). These contain information on what they each need to buy and what they each have to sell. Emphasize that in conducting negotiations they must stick to the rules of their culture as set out in their instructions. Give each person some currency, e.g. counters, pebbles or sweets, and allow them ten minutes to see how well they can do. Hand out the cards showing items for sale to the relevant person. Observe the situations to ensure that the rules are being followed. Teams are free to buy and sell at what ever price they wish. As no one is likely to do a deal, the cost of items becomes irrelevant. After the game is over get feedback. If all has gone to plan, very few people will have got what they needed.

• Why is that?

In the game, the rules of each tribe are such that it is almost impossible to trade at all. From your experience of this simple exercise it's clear to see that in order for trading to take place the rules would need to be changed so that everyone has an opportunity to get what they need.

The trade rules that exist in our world are also unpractical, not because of cultural reasons, but because they were written by rich and powerful nations and therefore work to their benefit. They are unfair, but because we don't really experience the impact in our everyday lives many of us trade on regardless.

• •

Breakfast is served (5 mins)

The dictionary defines trade as 'buying and selling'. Trade is the way we overcome shortage in resources within communities, regions and nations. Fair business transactions are essential to distribute the benefits of God's goodness between individuals and nations. There are loads of famous sayings of Martin Luther King, but ask your group what they think he meant when he said: 'Before you sit down to breakfast you will have relied on half the world.'

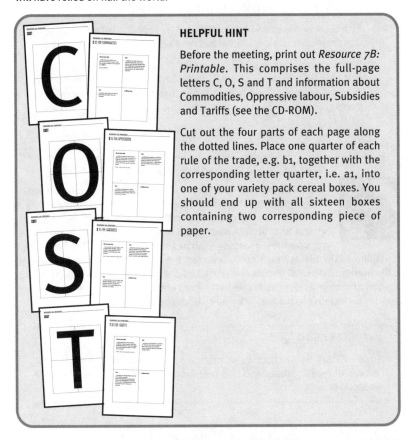

HELPFUL HINT

Before the meeting, print out *Resource 7B: Printable*. This comprises the full-page letters C, O, S and T and information about Commodities, Oppressive labour, Subsidies and Tariffs (see the CD-ROM).

Cut out the four parts of each page along the dotted lines. Place one quarter of each rule of the trade, e.g. b1, together with the corresponding letter quarter, i.e. a1, into one of your variety pack cereal boxes. You should end up with all sixteen boxes containing two corresponding piece of paper.

Hand out your variety pack of cereals and use them to discuss where people think the different ingredients may have come from. Almost everything we buy brings a global dimension to our lives, from the flex on our kettles and the fuel in our cars, to the food on our plates. So why is it that poor countries remain poor? Trade can force people into poverty or lift them out of it. Practised fairly, it can create opportunities for employment and profitable livelihoods. However, the rules of trade set up by the World Trade Organization largely reflect the interests of the rich governments and the large corporate identities who dominate it.

They [World Trade Organization] argue for free trade, yet erect barriers against imports from developing countries. They argue for rules, yet abuse anti-dumping or health and safety legislation to unfairly restrict imports. They support development, but then deter countries from processing their own products by tariff escalation.' [72]

FACE FACTS

- Africa loses the equivalent of 50 pence for every pound received in aid because of the falling prices it gets for its commodities.

- Rich countries spend $1 billion a day on agricultural subsidies, putting farmers in poor countries out of business and driving down their income.

- For every dollar given to poor countries in aid, they lose two dollars to rich countries because of unfair trade barriers against their exports. Producers in poor countries pay tariffs that are four times higher than those paid by producers in other rich countries.

Source: Make Trade Fair

Free trade, but at what C.O.S.T.? (20 mins)

Current trade rules make it hard for poor countries to develop and to escape poverty. They are complicated, but the following exercise should help your group to understand their impact. Divide into four groups and allocate each group one area of trade to focus on, i.e. commodities, oppressive labour, subsidies and tariffs. Each group must find all the pieces of their puzzle among the various cereal boxes in order to build up their individual picture of trade. Hand out glue and ask them to paste one quarter of each individual trade rule to the front of their box and the corresponding quarter of the letter to the back. They should end up with three boxes per group.

IMPORTANT INFO

For now, keep hold of the box for each rule containing the quarter marked 'A different way'. Groups will find that without it, the trade rules literally won't stack up!

TRADE — A DIFFERENT WAY . . .

Globally – God rules OK (15 mins)

Read Isaiah 10:1–2 together and ask for people's reactions. Ask each group to think about what they have discovered through the session and to discuss and pray about what changes God might require to make trade fairer for all. Using the blank block or final piece of their puzzle, ask each group to think up a rule which might mean trade was more just. If they are struggling, suggest the following as possible solutions:

- COMMODITIES: Poor countries need to be able to negotiate fair prices for their raw materials.

● OPPRESSION: The rights of the poorest, most vulnerable people in the world need protecting. Multinational companies must be held accountable for every stage of production of their goods.

● SUBSIDIES (on goods from developed countries): Rich countries should end the export subsidies that damage the livelihoods of poor countries around the world.

● TARIFFS (on goods entering developing countries): Poor countries should have the freedom to choose policies that support their small-scale farmers and industries so that they can compete with imports.

Nationally – trade justice

Call on the government to rewrite trade rules. Show how you've considered trade and say what you think works and what doesn't. Send off a letter, or even better, one of your cereal boxes, and mail it to the Prime Minister for him to consider during his breakfast-time reading. Check out www.tearfund.org/trade for the latest campaign information.

Locally – fair trade

Buying goods that are fairly traded is just one way you can impact global trade on a personal level. Purchasing Fairtrade products guarantees that producers:

● are paid a price that covers the costs of sustainable production and living

● are paid a 'premium' that they are able invest in development, e.g. improving their homes, improving education and healthcare, building roads, investing in their businesses or diversifying into other income-generating projects

● may request partial advance payments

● are able to sign contracts that allow for long-term planning and sustainable production practices.

As a group, why not think about how in just one week you could make changes to trade:

● **Friday:** Try out a few Fairtrade recipes with your group. Visit www.fairtrade.org.uk/resources_recipes.htm for some ideas.

● **Saturday:** Ask for permission to organize a tasting stand at your local supermarket. Hand out free food and talk to people about Fairtrade. (Asda, Budgens, Booths, Co-op, Morrisons, Sainsburys, Safeway, Somerfield, Spar, Tesco and Waitrose all currently sell Fairtrade products.)

● **Sunday:** Ask for a prayer slot or a perhaps prepare a short talk on Fairtrade for your church meeting.

● **Monday:** Arrange a Fairtrade stall at school. Show people what products are available – see if you can get some freebies for tasting from Fairtrade stockists.

- **Tuesday**: Commit to buying Fairtrade chocolate from now on. There are loads to choose from, including Chocaid, Co-op, Divine, Dubble, Green & Blacks, Tesco and Traidcraft.

- **Wednesday**: Ask your school, college or university whether they would be prepared to switch to Fairtrade. Visit www.tearfund.org/liftthelabel for more info. A list of suppliers is available from www.fairtrade.org.uk/suppliers.htm.

- **Thursday**: Hold a Fairtrade party using only Fairtrade food and drinks. Encourage your group to ask their parents/carers to try out some Fairtrade products at home (either items they've cooked or purchased).

HELPFUL HINT

You could become a Fairtrade church by meeting the following goals:

- Use Fairtrade tea and coffee for all meetings for which we have responsibility.

- Move forward on using other Fairtrade products, such as sugar, biscuits and fruit.

- Promote Fairtrade at events during Fairtrade Fortnight – and through other activities, whenever possible.

Alternatively, if you were able to meet the following goals, you could become a Fairtrade town:

- The local council must pass a resolution supporting Fairtrade and must serve Fairtrade coffee and tea at its meetings and in offices and canteens.

- A range of Fairtrade products must be readily available in the area's shops and served in local cafés and catering establishments (targets are set in relation to population).

- Fairtrade products must be used by a number of local work places (estate agents, hairdressers, etc.) and community organizations (churches, schools, etc.).

- The council must attract popular support for the campaign.

- A local Fairtrade steering group must be convened to ensure continued commitment to Fairtrade Town status.

Download an application form to become a Fairtrade church at www.tearfund.org/trade or check out those who have already become Fairtrade towns at www.fairtrade.org.uk.[73]

THE DIFFERENT ISSUES...
DEBT

Sub-Saharan Africa receives $10 billion in aid every year – but has to pay back at least this amount in debt repayments.[74] Why is this? Well, way back in the 1960s and 1970s poorer countries were encouraged to borrow money from the West. Unfortunately, much of this money was unwisely invested in short-term, often destructive projects that had no real benefit for the majority of the country's population. A rise in interest rates during the late 1970s and the 1980s means that even after years of repaying their debts, many countries now owe *more* than their original loans. This huge burden of debt prevents them from spending much-needed money on things like education, water and sanitation, and other basic services.

FACE FACTS

● Malawi is just one of many countries which spends more on servicing its debt, i.e. repaying interest, than it does on such essentials as health, despite the fact that nearly one in five Malawians are HIV positive.

● Zambia's debt repayments to the IMF are currently $25 million, which is more than it spends on education, even though 40 percent of rural women are unable to read and write.

● If we are to reach the Millennium Development Goal of halving the number of people living on less than 60 pence a day by 2015, we must cancel all the debts of the poorest countries.

Source: Jubilee Debt Campaign

In an attempt to reduce the debts of poorer countries, in 1996 the World Bank and the IMF set up the Heavily Indebted Poor Countries (HIPC) initiative. The HIPC is a scheme that, amongst other things, is designed to help poorer nations to prioritize their debt repayments – unfortunately this is often ahead of much needed spending on health and education. So far only 18 countries, out of a possible 42 who qualify, have reached 'Completion Point' and received some debt cancellation. These countries are: Benin, Bolivia, Burkina Faso, Ethiopia, Ghana, Guyana, Honduras, Madagascar, Mali, Mauritania, Mozambique, Nicaragua, Niger, Rwanda, Senegal, Tanzania, Uganda and Zambia.

According to President Mkapa of Tanzania, if countries like these are ever going to fight poverty and win, all their debts must be wiped out. So far debt relief in Tanzania has resulted in the building of more than 2000 schools and a 66 percent increase in the number of children in primary school. Further improvements in things such as secondary education, healthcare and water provision – things that could save thousands of lives – will only be possible with further relief. In short, he says: 'Give us the tools and we will finish the job.'

Recently the UK agreed to cancel the debts that are owed to it directly (bilateral debt), by 27 countries involved in the HIPC process. That includes the 18 countries that have completed the HIPC process, plus a further nine countries that have reached 'Decision Point', the first stage of the initiative.[75] It has also pledged an extra £100 million a year, up until 2015, to cover all debt service payments owed to it through lenders such as the World Bank and the African Development Bank. Unfortunately under the current proposals any debt that remains after this date will have to be paid back.

Do the maths: 42 qualifiers, less 27 still leaves 15. The remaining 15 indebted countries eligible for the HIPC process must continue to repay their debts until they reach stage one of the process – if they ever do.[76] Add to this those poorer countries currently receiving no debt relief, such as Bangladesh and Nigeria, and it's clear that debt relief has the potential to lift or leave millions of people out of or in poverty. It's essential that all unpayable debts must be cancelled, in full, without damaging restrictions. Furthermore the cancellation must be funded from new money, not from sneaky tricks where rich nations take it out of the aid they have promised poor countries.

SESSION 8
DEBT

Aim: To understand the concept of debt and see how it is a major factor in keeping poor people in poverty; just like rewriting international trade rules, cancelling unpayable debt is essential if poverty is ever to be eradicated.

You will need: One copy of *Resource 8A: Printable*, currency (e.g. counters, sweets, etc.), timing device, scissors, pens or pencils, paper, various shape templates, one copy of *Resource 8B: Worksheet, Resource 8C: Case study*, Bibles, one copy of *Resource 8D: Drama*, various items costing around £3 each, camera.

Interest free? (20 mins)

The idea of the game is to understand a little about how we can get into debt. Divide your group into two or three smaller groups, handing the instructions to the relevant teams (*Resource 8A: Printable*).

- Group one (which, if you prefer, is a role that as a leader you could play) represents one of the rich G8 countries – USA, UK, Japan, Canada, Russia, France, Italy or Germany.

- Groups two and three represent poorer countries of the world.

Explain that the aim of the game is to 'Improve the education, health services and infrastructure (by this we mean roads, buildings, etc.) of your country'.

1. Before the game begins, groups two and three must decide whether to:

- buy equipment – at two units per item

- borrow money – agreeing to pay back four units for every one they borrow at the end of the round

- bank and invest in education, health or infrastructure – costing six units each.

2. After two minutes, groups two and three must hand over all their equipment, repay their debts if they can, and decide whether to:

- buy equipment for the next round – at four units per item

- borrow more money – agreeing to pay back six units for every one they borrow at the end of the round

- bank and invest in education, health or infrastructure – costing eight units each.

3. After a further two minutes, groups two and three must hand over all their equipment, repay their debts, and decide whether to:

● buy equipment for the next round – at six units per item

● borrow more money – agreeing to pay back eight units for every one they borrow at the end of the round

● bank and invest in education, health or infrastructure – costing ten units each.

4. After a further two minutes, groups two and three must hand over all their equipment, work out what they've made, how much they owe in debts and how much they've invested in health, education and infrastructure (which of course was the original aim of the game).

At the end of the game, take feedback.

● Can you remember the original aim of the game? Were you successful?

● How did the process make you feel?

● In what ways did borrowing more money help/not help you?

HELPFUL HINT

Emphasize that the original aim of the game was to keep the education and health services of each country going; to do that they needed money. Chances are, each group will have forgotten this once they got engrossed in the game. Eventually it would become impossible to survive without borrowing money.

● ●

Step by step (10 mins)

Copy, cut out and mix up the statements about debt (*Resource 8B: Worksheet 3*), and ask your group to put them in sequence. Note how education and health suffer as a result of bad investment and growing debt, just as they did in the first game!

● ●

The way ahead? (10 mins)

Set up in 1996 by the World Bank and the IMF, the Heavily Indebted Poor Countries (HIPC) initiative – the current scheme for international debt relief – has received much criticism. Not only does it demand cuts in health and education spending, but it protects the assets and interests of creditors rather than promote growth, poverty-reduction or stability and it undermines the democracy of poorer countries by denying elected parliaments or civil society a say in important decisions about how the country is run.[77] It is also said to be:

● **Too long**: so far only 18 countries have been able to complete the HIPC process (reached 'Completion Point') and received some debt cancellation.[78] A further nine countries have reached the first stage ('Decision Point'), at which point they receive some relief on debt repayments.[79]

● **Too little**: rather than cancelling debts, the scheme only reduces them to a level that the creditors claim to be 'sustainable'. As a result, even countries that have completed the process still struggle to meet their debt repayments and have to divert money from vital public services.

● **Too limited**: Only 42 countries are 'eligible', and out of these only 27 have even qualified for eventual debt cancellation through the scheme. Some of the others are never likely to qualify for any debt relief at all.[80] A number of other countries, such as Bangladesh, Nigeria and Peru, are equally poor and heavily indebted, but do not meet the World Bank and IMF criteria that would enable them to qualify as HIPCs.

Consider the following case study (*Resource 8C: Case study*).

PEOPLE AND POVERTY

CASE STUDY – UGANDA

Kigutua Primary School, in south-west Uganda, started life under a group of trees in 1985. Back then, 55 pupils took shelter from the elements to have their lessons. As time passed, the school moved into some mud buildings and the pupils increased to 425. The school made progress, gradually building up its reputation, though the site became waterlogged easily, causing the latrines to swamp the compound and playground. Teachers, parents and pupils made the best of the situation, however, and eventually their efforts started to pay off.

In 2001, Uganda received debt relief because millions of people across the world urged the G8 leaders, the World Bank and International Monetary Fund to take action. The government of Uganda used the extra money to fund the building of two classrooms, a store, an office and new latrines at Kigutua. Most of the parents didn't know what debt relief was, but they eagerly helped with the building work. Their children now have a safe place to study and clean sanitation at school, and the teachers have a better environment in which to do their jobs.

Source: Tearfund

Please release me (20 mins)

Read Deuteronomy 15:1–11 together. Explain the concept behind releasing people from debt and ask:

● In what circumstances would you allow someone to keep something that belonged to you or that they owed you?

● In what ways would your feelings depend on how much it meant to you or who it was?

● What are the positives and negatives of simply 'letting people off'?

● What do you understand by being 'open-handed'?

● Explain why you think God made this law?

BIBLICAL BACKGROUND

The cancelling of debts gave Israelites who had experienced economic hardship the chance to start again. In order to find their way out of poverty, a person who is poor may need to get into debt. Deuteronomy 15 contains good advice on lending to the poor in a way that preserves their dignity. The Old Testament strictly prohibits charging interest on loans to the poor. Deuteronomy 15 emphasizes the need for a cut-off point, i.e. lender cannot extract repayments indefinitely. In real terms, much of what poor countries owe in terms of debt today is in interest rather than what they originally borrowed.

DEBT – A DIFFERENT WAY...

Globally – promises, promises

Use the drama about debt (*Resource 8D: Drama*) to reflect on how developing world debt came about. Use this to stimulate an open time of prayer.

● ●

Nationally – promises, promises

In 1996, inspired by the biblical year of Jubilee, in which debts and grievances were forgiven and prisoners were released, more than 70 organizations including aid agencies, church groups, trade unions and many others formed a coalition that proposed a one-off cancellation of the unpayable debt of developing countries by the year 2000. 24.3 million people from 160 countries signed the petition and, in just four years, international debt was forced to the top of the political agenda. Successive campaign actions at G8 summits since have increased public awareness of the debt situation of the world's poorest countries. Despite the eloquent summit promises by the UK government and others, more than 85 percent of the debt owed by the world's poorest countries still remains. Countries that have had some of their debt cancelled have benefited.

FACE THE FACTS

Spending on education in some African countries is now twice as much as is being spent on debt repayments. Spending on health has risen by 70 percent and is now one-third more than is being spent on debt.

● In Tanzania, debt relief has enabled the government to abolish primary school fees, leading to a 66 percent increase in attendance.

● In Benin, 54 percent of the money saved through debt relief has been spent on health, including on rural primary healthcare and HIV programmes.

● After Mozambique was granted debt relief, it was able to offer all children free immunization.

● In Uganda, debt relief led to 2.2 million people gaining access to water.

Cancelling debt has made a difference to the lives of many people, but too many countries are still spending money on servicing debts instead of on health, education and clean water. Without 100 percent debt cancellation, there is little hope of these countries meeting the 2015 Millennium Development Goals set by the United Nations General Assembly at the start of the new millennium. Tearfund continues to work with the Jubilee Debt Campaign, as it did with Jubilee 2000, towards the cancellation of the majority world debt.

Source: Tearfund and Jubilee Debt Campaign

Visit www.jubileedebtcampaign.org.uk for the latest ways to take action.

Locally – £3

As well as the debts they owe to other countries, the 42 HIPCs also owe money to multilaterals such as the World Bank, the IMF and the African Development Bank. The current cost of cancelling the UK's 'share' of these debts would be a little as £3 per person per year over ten years (or a one off payment of £30).[81] Over the next week, ask each individual to look out for a product that costs about £3. Ask them to bring them along to your next session. Take a photo of each person holding their object and encourage them to either write a prayer, a challenge to themselves, or maybe even a note of encouragement to the Chancellor of the Exchequer asking him to continue his efforts to bring about debt relief for poorer countries.

HELPFUL HINT

You could use a Polaroid and write messages along the bottom strip, or use a digital camera and produce a PowerPoint presentation. Perhaps show it to the wider group you're part of and get them involved, for example your church, school or college.

You could make a start this week by listing the kinds of things people in the group think might cost this amount. Finish and pray through some of the issues covered during the session.

● What would it mean for you to give these kinds of things up?

● What would it mean for people in debt if the Chancellor felt sufficiently challenged to increase his current promises to drop the debt and put pressure on other nations to do the same?

● Ask God to reveal to you what else you could do to relieve crippling debts.

THE DIFFERENT ISSUES...
AID

Believe it or not an incredible $70 billion is currently spent on international aid each year. This is delivered either bilaterally – from one country to another – or multilaterally – through organizations such as the World Bank – or via mechanisms such as the Global Fund to fight AIDS, TB and Malaria. However, with more than one billion people in the world still living in extreme poverty, more assistance is required if they are ever to reach a point where they are able to lift themselves out of poverty.

In a fallen world, humanity's pursuit of wealth has led to great inequality and broken relationships between nations as well as individuals. Although half the world lives comfortably, how the other half lives can only be described as abject poverty – surely not life as God intended. Transferring wealth, in the form of international development aid, on which no interest is charged, is just one way we can return a sense of equality to our different world.

Aid has nothing to do with charity and everything to do with justice. It's our responsibility to hold our leaders accountable for the wealth that they control and to remind them of their responsibility toward the poor. We not only need to urge our leaders to give more to the poor, but aid needs to be delivered in a way that provides long-term and sustainable solutions to poverty, and with minimal harm to the environment. Poor people should be encouraged and enabled to participate in deciding how aid can be spent in ways that will be of benefit to them.

MORE AID

More than 30 years ago, rich countries such as the UK agreed to give 0.7 percent of their income away as aid. Only a handful of countries have stuck to their promise: the UK isn't one.[82] The UK Government has made a commitment to increase its aid budget to 0.51 percent of its Gross National Income (GNI) by 2010, and promised to meet the 0.7 percent target by 2013, but that would only leave two years to accomplish the Millennium Development Goals and halve world poverty. Tearfund is one of many organizations that believes that at least another $50 billion in international aid needs to be made available every year.

> **FACE FACTS**
>
> To achieve 0.7 percent, the UK needs to increase its aid budget by £3 billion. It sounds huge, but it is possible – the UK government found £5.5 billion to fund the 'war on terror'.[83]

BETTER AID

As well as more aid, aid needs to work better for poorer communities than it currently does. The most vulnerable people in our world are not always the ones that benefit from aid in the way you might expect, for some of the following reasons:

- **Politics:** Much of the aid given to poorer countries tends to be given to the political allies of richer nations rather than those who need it most. In 2001 only 38 percent of the EU's development aid went to low income and least developed countries, with 62 percent going to middle income countries. More formal tracking procedures are required in order to ensure that international aid reaches its intended beneficiaries.

- **Economics:** The World Bank, IMF and bilateral donors often provide aid in return for trading practices that tend to work in favour of richer nations and to the detriment of the poor. If poor countries are ever going to gain control over their own futures and see aid as an effective tool for poverty eradication, economic policy conditions need to be abandoned.

- **Ownership:** Decisions about how international aid is spent are often imposed by universal approaches and policies made by the institutions and donors who give it rather than the local people who need it. Donors ought to be supporting policies and strategies based on national choices that better reflect the priorities of poor people.

- **Sustainability:** Lack of certainty about when, how much and for how long a country might expect to receive international aid makes planning for the future difficult. There are always going to be situations in which the provision of immediate short-term emergency aid is necessary, for example disasters. However, there is no doubt that aid is more effective if a higher proportion of it can be spent on long-term strategies that reduce the risks that vulnerable communities might face in the future. Disaster mitigation and preparedness designed to reduce the impact of future disasters is a much more cost-effective way of delivering a high-volume emergency relief.

More money is urgently required from governments than they currently contribute to international aid. However, unless the issues outlined above concerning the quality of that aid are also addressed, no amount of money will ever be sufficient enough to begin to address poverty in the way that it might.

SESSION 9
AID

Aim: To help individuals understand the way people in poverty are often living on the edge of survival. To see the need for aid and what we can do to ensure more and better aid is given.

You will need: Copies of *Resource 9A: Printable*, copies of *Resource 9B: Printable*, a dice, stapler, copies of *Resource 9C: Worksheet*, Bibles, pens, paper, *Resource 9D: Printable*, *Resource 9E: Interactive*.

Beyond bad hair (10 mins)

Everyone has their off days, when they feel as though the world might as well end because nothing is going right.

Think of some 'personal disasters' as a group, for example having a bad hair day, losing your keys, splitting up with your boy/girlfriend. (Be sensitive and try and keep it light-hearted.)

Discuss how bad it felt at the time, then for each one estimate how long it took you to get over it.

What about real disasters? Ones that have devastating life-threatening consequences for those involved? Ask your group to recall the last natural disaster reported on the news. Print off some of the quotes from *Resource 9A: Printable* if you feel that these might help to stimulate people's thinking (see CD-ROM).

● Try to recall your immediate reaction to a recent global disaster. As a group, share how and why you felt the way you did.

● What about those actually involved, how must they have felt? (The following exercise might help.)

● ●

Lifeline (20 mins)

Print off a copy of *Resource 9B: Printable* for each member of your group. Cut out the strips and place them in a pile in the centre of your room/the group. Each person should take turns throwing a die and picking up a strip from the pile depending on the number they get. You must throw a 1 to start. For example:

● Throw a 1, get – food

● Throw a 2, get – health

● Throw a 3, get – clothes

- Throw a 4, get – job/education
- Throw a 5, get – house
- Throw a 6 – lose everything!

Link the strips together using a stapler to form a chain, starting with number 1 and placing them in numerical order. If anyone throws a 6 or any number in succession their chain is destroyed and they have to start all over again. The winner is the person with the longest chain after five minutes (or the length of time you decide to spend on the game).

The point is that no matter how much or little people living in poverty have, when disaster strikes, whether that be a natural hazard, war or disease, they generally have no back-up plan, no insurance, no security and sometimes no way back.

• •

What a relief (10 mins)

In response to the tsunami in 2004, the British government pledged more than £100 million,[84] and the British public donated £250 million[85]– but what was it used for? Print off *Resource 9C: Worksheet 3* and ask people to guess the estimated cost of each of the essential items. The answers are: 16p, £1.30, £50 and £105. Think about what a difference your money could make as agencies work to rebuild communities throughout areas in need, in this case Sri Lanka. The need for aid in times of disaster is a matter of life or death, but don't just think it's about one-off disasters. As Prime Minister Tony Blair said after the tsunami of 2004, 'There's a manmade tsunami in Africa every day'.

In fact 30,000 children die daily because of preventable disease and poor sanitation, 6800 of them from diarrhoea alone.[86] World poverty is sustained not by chance or nature, but by a combination of factors: injustice in global trade; the huge burden of debt; corruption; insufficient and ineffective aid. So what are we prepared to do about it?

• •

First aid, then...? (10 mins)

God hates the fact that people made in his image are fighting just to survive. He hates it that children are robbed of a future because they cannot get basic healthcare or education. So he commands us to act. Read Luke 10:25–37 together, the parable of the Good Samaritan.

- As you read, list all the verbs in the passage, i.e. the 'doing' words.
- At the end of the reading, categorize all the words into positive action and negative action.

Take feedback and then use the following questions to begin to unpack our responsibility towards people in need of aid.

- In what ways was the man in the story in need?
- In what ways was he prevented from helping himself?
- What kind of things do you imagine caused the passers-by to pass by?

BIBLICAL BACKGROUND

THE PRIEST AND THE LEVITE

Lots of people got mugged on that road; it wasn't safe to stop and get involved. How did they know if the man lying there really was mugged? Is he just pretending, waiting for someone to stop so his friends can jump out and mug the next fool?

The religious people were too busy, too self-absorbed, too scared to stop and see. They needed to be 'clean' to do their day jobs.

● What caused the Samaritan to stop? In what ways would it have been easier to walk on by like the others?

● Why would it have been so hard for the crowd Jesus was addressing to accept that it was the Samaritan that eventually stopped to help out?

BIBLICAL BACKGROUND

THE SAMARITAN

He was the wrong person: wrong race and wrong religion. Jews and Samaritans hated each other. The Samaritans were held in contempt as religious rebels who had mixed the purity of Israel's worship with idolatry and the worship of pagan gods (2 Kgs. 17:24–41; the Apocrypha book of Sirach 50:25–26). The animosity toward the Samaritans was greatly intensified about 20 years before Jesus's ministry when some Samaritans defiled the temple in Jerusalem by scattering human bones in the courtyard during Passover (Josephus Antiquities of the Jews 18.30). This conflict at the temple highlights one of the fundamental differences between the Samaritans and the Jews, namely, the question of where God has centred his worship.[87] The people listening to Jesus tell this story probably spat and groaned and swore when he mentioned a Samaritan.

● What sort of things did the Samaritan do? What did it cost him?

• •

Go and do likewise (10 mins)

It's sometimes easy to get so wrapped up in the story of the Good Samaritan that we actually forget the reason Jesus told the story in the first place. He told it in response to a question '...who is my neighbour?' which came from a lawyer (Lk. 10:29). Jesus' answer is simple: anyone! So who is the neighbour you're commanded to love? Answer: whoever needs you to be. We can't limit our compassion – who we have to love and who we can ignore. We must show mercy to those who need mercy; love to those who need love; aid to those who are in need. Love is, after all, a verb, a 'doing' word.

- Think about the needs around you. Categorize them into local, national and global.

- What stops you from stopping to help?

- In what ways would people benefit if you did? In what ways would you benefit/lose out if you did?

- Spend some time in reflection and praying before thinking about your response.

HELPFUL HINT

More and better aid is needed. Way back in 1970 the UN set a target for all developed nations that would make a huge difference to the amounts of aid around. It suggested that governments give 0.7 percent of what they make each year. It's not a lot, is it? So why does the UK government currently give only 0.34 percent? Unless rich countries like the UK honour their pledge of 0.7 percent, poor nations will not be unable to meet the UN MDGs by 2015. The result will be millions of people who will have died through insufficient aid.

AID – A DIFFERENT WAY...

Locally – fun raising

You've seen what your money can do, so why not raise some? Here are a few favourite fundraising tips. *Resource 9D: Printable* is a sponsor form that can be used for any of these events.

- **Snub the grub.** What about 24 hours without food? No? Then try not eating cake, chocolate or salad and send the money you save to relief and development agencies such as Tearfund.

- **Bored? Not sporty?** Well, try a sponsored games night – table football, Monopoly or any other board game of your choice. Of course, there are always consoles and computer games for the armchair sports fan.

- **It's a dog's life.** If you're going to walk, you might as well take a dog. Earn some cash off your neighbours by volunteering to exercise their pampered pooches.

- **Invest in the best.** Take a pound and invest it. Bake it, make it, wrap it – there's always a market for good cakes, cards, crafts and present wrapping, particularly around Easter and Christmas.

- **Hit, miss or maybe not?** Hidden talents? Set up a talent night, concert or ball and invite people to pay for the privilege of making fools of themselves. Karaoke is always a favourite, especially for those people who really shouldn't consider singing in public.

Globally – life aid

Why not commit to give 0.7 percent of your own income to the long-term work of development charities such as Tearfund? Use the 'Aid adder' (*Resource 9E: Interactive,* separate file on CD Rom) to work out how much this would mean, both individually and maybe as a group. Visit www.tearfund.org/liftthelabel/finance for more information, or, provided you are already online use the 'check here for more...' facility on the final screen of 'Aid Adder'.

• •

Nationally – I will: will you?

Ask the UK government to provide more and better aid. You could either challenge your MP to ensure that both the UK and other countries match your generosity or write to the Chancellor of the Exchequer saying 'I'm giving 0.7 percent, please will you?' Visit www.tearfund.org/liftthelabel for more information.

A DIFFERENT CONCLUSION
A HEART FOR THE POOR

You probably didn't need a big thick book to help you to see that you live in a different world; a quick glance at some of the images of poverty which appear in the evening news, your half-read newspaper or your daily e-mails ought to be enough to convince you that the world is full of inequality and injustice. But how connected to the issues do you really feel, or do the images begin to disappear from your mind even before you've switched channel, turned the page, closed the file or read the book?

Why is it that 100 percent of the UK population (60 million people) has access to clean drinking water, whilst 75 percent of the population of Ethiopia doesn't – that's 45 million people. Twenty-one million mobile phones are owned by 14–25-year olds in the UK, yet over five billion people in the world don't even have access to reliable landlines. How can a Premiership footballer earn tens of thousand of pounds a day while children in the developing world are expected to work 16 hour shifts for less than 60p a day stitching boots? Whether or not you've heard facts like these before you used this book, you've probably always questioned whether this is how things are meant to be.

The real question for you, however, is how do such opposing facts from two sides of our different world inform our life from here on in? Perhaps a double act of worship and justice could make all the difference to the way we live our lives. In Isaiah 58, God gives us a glimpse at the kind of worshipful lifestyle he expects of his people. The Jews were doing all the right things – praying, fasting, worshipping and all that stuff – but nothing seemed to happen. 'Why have we fasted,' they say, 'and you have not seen it? Why have we humbled ourselves, and you have not noticed?' (Is. 58:3).

God never seemed to answer their prayers; they constantly missed his will and felt as far away from him as they had ever done – why? Through Isaiah, God reveals three major things for them to work on, and as worshippers eager to lead others closer to him, we need to bear these in mind too.

WORSHIP WITH INTEGRITY

God questions Israel's integrity. They pray one thing but they do the opposite. '...on the day of your fasting, you do as you please and exploit all your workers. Your fasting ends in quarrelling and strife, and in striking each other with wicked fists. You cannot fast as you do today and expect your voice to be heard on high' (Is. 58:3–5).

We need to ask ourselves whether we really worship with integrity. What injustice in our own lives can't disappear by simply shutting our eyes to pray or raising our hands to worship? Or, as a friend once said to me: 'how do you expect God to answer your prayers whilst you're wearing those trainers?' Even if I pray or sing against injustice daily, do my lifestyle choices echo my demands? Do the trainers I wear, or the snacks I consume, contribute to or combat the injustice I pray about? Have people really been treated fairly in providing for my lifestyle? Which screams loudest to God, my words or my actions? Presumably, rather than just songs, what God really wants is a 'just' lifestyle full of activity that benefits others.

WORSHIP THROUGH ACTION

More than any heartfelt song, God seems to be calling for radical action to change the way people are treated. Imagine how a friend would feel if they asked you to help them carry a piano down 58 flights of stairs and all you did was stand at the bottom, sing songs, praise their efforts and say how awesome they were. Is that how to show you honour someone, that when they ask something of us, we'd rather worship from afar than roll our sleeves up and get stuck in? How does God feel when he asks us to show mercy and justice and all we do is sing?

> *Is not this the kind of fasting I have chosen: to loose the chains of injustice and untie the cords of the yoke, to set the oppressed free and break every yoke? Is it not to share your food with the hungry and to provide the poor wanderer with shelter – when you see the naked, to clothe him, and not to turn away from your own flesh and blood? (Is. 58:6–7)*

WORSHIP AS LIFESTYLE

What God wants from us is a life-long commitment to worship him and in doing so to love others: a life that doesn't just speak about a desire to 'loose the chains of injustice' but actually does it. God wants a life emptied, given over and completely spent for the sake of someone other than ourselves. It's hard to dispute that God is into justice, or that he requires us to be too, so perhaps the question for us ought to be – how?

> *Spend yourselves on behalf of the hungry and satisfy the needs of the oppressed, then your light will rise in the darkness, and your night will become like the noonday ... you will be called Repairer of Broken Walls, Restorer of Streets with Dwellings. (Is. 58:10–12)*

So how do we maintain the worship/life balance? So what does God want? He wants 'just' worship and a 'just' life. A life that is full of worship, but not any old worship, worship that is simple, plain and more effective because it is fair, right, impartial, honest, honourable, righteous, moral and truthful. Most of all, he wants worship that informs our choices and that makes a difference to him, to us, for others and for good.

SESSION 10
A HEART FOR THE POOR

Aim: To grasp God's heart for the poor and what we as individuals need to do about global poverty in response. Faced with so much need, what is our understanding of what God thinks about it and what we need to do about it?

You will need: Pens, paper, copies of *Resource 10A: Printable*, copy of *Resource 10B: Printable*, balls of coloured wool, Bibles, *Resource 10C: Printable*.

THE POVERTY GAP (10 mins)

Print off *Resource 10A: Printable*. This represents the contrasting experiences of people living in poverty and people such as ourselves. Hand out one fact to each individual and ask them to find someone else with a matching, but opposing fact to theirs. Alternatively, distribute the cards randomly and ask people to match up the contrasting facts, placing them in two columns like so:

Nobody in the UK is expected to live on less than 60p a day.[88]	72 percent of the population of Mali live on less than 60p a day.[89]
0.1 percent of 15–49 year olds in the UK are living with HIV and AIDS.[90]	39 percent of 15–49 year olds in Botswana are living with HIV and AIDS.[91]
In the UK 100 percent of the population has access to clean drinking water.[92]	In Cambodia just 30 percent of the population has access to clean drinking water.[93]
100 percent of the population of the UK enrol for primary education.[94]	Just 16 percent of the population of Bhutan enrol for primary education.[95]
In the UK, 99 percent of adults above the age of 15 years are literate.[96]	In Niger just 15 percent of adults above the age of 15 years are literate.[97]
The average life expectancy in the UK is 78 years.[98]	The average life expectancy in Sierra Leone is just 39 years.[99]
In 2000, the average annual income in the UK was £14,968.[100]	In 2000, the average annual income in Tanzania was £333.[101]
Every year in the UK about £1700 is spent on each person's healthcare.[102]	Every year in Ethiopia about £4 is spent on each person's healthcare.[103]
In 2001 people in the UK spent £800 million on coffee.[104]	The average grower receives just 5p out of the £1.75 you pay for your cappuccino.[105]
In the UK, for every 1000 live births, 4 die before they reach a year old.[106]	In Angola, for every 1000 live births, 172 die before they reach a year old.[107]
727 in every 1000 people in the UK own a mobile phone.[108]	In Cuba, just one in every 1000 people owns a mobile phone.[109]

Whole hearted (15 mins)

Spend some time considering God's response to the poverty gap. Create a heart shape on the floor using masking tape. Sit your group around the heart, facing inwards. Hand each person a pen or pencil, which they are to hold out in front of them.

Take one of the key words from *Resource 10B: Printable*, for example 'GIVE', 'SAVE'. Say it out loud, place it into the centre, and then encourage all the group to look at it and to think about (but not say) the first word that comes into their head. Hand one person a ball of coloured wool. The person holding the wool starts by sharing the first word that entered their head, wraps the wool five times around their pen and throws the wool to someone else in the group. That person must then say the first word that entered their head, wrap the wool around their pen five times, and throw it to someone else, and so on. If a person repeats another player's word or hesitates, they must throw the wool on without wrapping it around their pen. When you feel you've exhausted all the words associated with your initial key word, choose another key word and ask the person holding the wool to think of a word they first associate with that. Continue until you have created a reasonably strong-looking web, or you get bored.

> **HELPFUL HINT**
>
> If you have a large group split them down into smaller groups of six or nine to create a number of web-like structures.

Global connections (10 mins)

Ask for a volunteer who might be prepared to lie on the structure to see if it will support them as the group attempts to lift them up off the floor. Swap places with them, taking hold of their pen. If the structure is complete enough it will support them. As it does, explain that the key words at the centre are all words in the Bible that express how God feels about the poor; if you like, they represent 'God's heart for the poor'. God's intention towards poor people is always positive, always proactive, always uplifting. We may think of the heart in terms of a feeling or emotion, but in the Bible the heart refers to the whole person, it is the very centre of their being. It's important to understand that the heart is about doing and not just about feelings. God acts on his feelings: he can never be described as half-hearted; action and feelings are inseparable for him. God feels so passionate about injustice that he does something about it – through Moses, prophets such as Amos and Isaiah, and ultimately through sending his son, Jesus. Colossians 1:15 talks about Jesus in terms of being a visible likeness of an invisible God – Jesus is God, in action, on earth.

> **HELPFUL HINT**
>
> Refer back to the poverty trap in session one, and suggest that, rather than allowing poverty to trap the poor, God's intention is for us to stand by them and support them as together we seek the best ways to end their poverty.

Mission possible? (10 mins)

So what did Jesus do in response to the poor? Place the following questions at intervals around the room:

1 What did Jesus say he had come to do?

2 How do we know that Jesus cared for people's physical needs?

3 What did Jesus say about how we should treat others?

4 How do we show we are Christians?

Divide the group into threes and hand out the following verses:

1 Matthew 20:28; Luke 4:18; John 10:10

2 Matthew 9:35–36; Matthew 15:32; Mark 1:40–42; Luke 7:12–15

3 Matthew 5:43–48; Luke 10:36–37; 1 John 3:17–18

4 Luke 6:35; Luke 19:8; James 2:14–17

Give them five minutes to place the right verse under the appropriate header question. Feedback and discuss the answers as a whole group.

> **BIBLICAL BACKGROUND**
>
> God is a God of justice and he loves poor people. In the Bible, one in every 16 verses concerns the poor: in Matthew, Mark and Luke it's one in every seven verses and in James it is one in every five. Do we need any more convincing that poor people are on God's agenda?

A HEART FOR THE POOR –
A DIFFERENT WAY...

Locally – in the short term (10 mins)

We've seen God's heart and Jesus's actions towards the poor, so what about us? As an initial response, reflect on a verse from the New Testament that makes clear our responsibility towards the poor in very simple and yet challenging terms: highlight Jesus's challenge to his disciples in John 14:12 – that they, and therefore as his disciple today, we would '...do even *greater* things.' It may sound a daunting prospect, an impossible task, but fear ought not to be an excuse for non-participation. Rather than be overwhelmed or discouraged, we ought to see picking up from where first God and then Jesus left off as a privilege.

Perhaps a good place to start to think about ways to begin to serve others would be to consider what it would mean for us to do some of the *same* things that Jesus did!

Get your group to lie down and close their eyes and encourage them to listen while you read out something that challenges them to consider what difference Jesus could make to their lives if they trust and allow him to have his way. Encourage them to think through Jesus's challenge to do even greater things – what would it be like if we saw the world the way God does?

CAN YOU SEE WHAT I SEE?

Tomorrow is a new day. It could prove to be the same as all the rest, but what if you had a choice for it to be different? You can either spend it as you always do, seeing what you've always seen, hearing what you always hear, feeling what you've always felt, or you could grasp a once-in-a-lifetime opportunity and accept God's offer of a loan of his senses.

What's in it for you? You may find that people seem to be shouting a little louder. You may even see things clearer than you did before; maybe even get your homework done faster. You may begin to find that you understand the opposite sex better and form more successful relationships in one day than you've ever had prior to this point. But is this short-term advance simply for your own sake?

Think of the difference it might make to everyone who knows you, or even those that don't. Would others feel, hear, see any difference in the way you relate to them when you're relying on God's senses more than your own? Would they find that you're listening more intensely? Would you stop twisting you're hair, folding your arms, twiddling your thumbs and maintain eye contact long enough to figure out whether the things coming out of their mouths are really worth being heard?

Of course, you may have already heard enough to convince you that a more permanent move of God's senses would be a better option than a one off loan. You'll take the eyes, the ears, even the heart of God – and you're prepared to use them.

And the catch? There's just a small one. On the odd occasion, perhaps not even that frequently at first, you may notice that as well as the places you want to go, you find yourself in situations that you've not really considered being part of before. Your regular places aren't off limits, but even they may not feel the same any more. Expect to start hanging out where God hangs out: with the orphaned, the diseased, the dying, the hungry and the starving. At first it may feel exciting, but it's only a matter of time before you can't help but match what you're sensing with some kind of responding. The demands may be small at first but soon enough you'll start to hear from everyone who's been desperate to be heard above the busyness that has become your life.

So what do you reckon? Can you do it? Now you understand a little of what it's like to glimpse at the world as God does, do you imagine it would ever look the same again? Now you've heard what God hears, would your world seem silent in comparison? Will feelings be a little empty without God's emotions? Will you hand back your insight, your newly found sense-ability? Will you pass over your God consciousness to someone who really cares?

Perhaps you feel like you've spent your whole life thus far searching and settling for *the next best thing*. Then why not grab this once-in-a-lifetime opportunity to experience *the next big thing* that God has in store for you. Before you finally decide to take permanent leave of just your own senses, remember this: when God hears, God does – when you hear, will you? When God sees, God does – when you see, will you? When God feels, God does – when you feel, will you?

Nationally – in the long term (10 mins)

In the Old Testament, Israel are reminded of what exactly it is that the Lord requires of them; it is simply: 'To act justly and to love mercy and to walk humbly...' (Mich. 6:8). The Micah Challenge is a campaign organized by the World Evangelical Alliance and the Micah Network (a group of more than 270 Christian organizations providing relief, development and justice ministries throughout the world) to mobilize Christians to act against poverty. The campaign aims to deepen Christian engagement with the poor and to influence leaders of rich and poor nations to fulfil their public promise to achieve the Millennium Development Goals (MDGs) and so halve absolute global poverty by 2015. The aim of the current challenge is to collect signatures representing more than 25 million individuals and more than a million local churches. The Micah Call is a powerful expression of support for achievement of the MDGs and the halving of poverty by 2015.

THE MICAH CALL

This is a moment in history of unique potential, when the stated intentions of world leaders echo something of the mind of the biblical prophets and the teachings of Jesus concerning the poor, and when we have the means to dramatically reduce poverty.

We commit ourselves, as followers of Jesus, to work together for the holistic transformation of our communities, to pursue justice, be passionate about kindness and to walk humbly with God.

We call on international and national decision-makers of both rich and poor nations, to fulfil their public promise to achieve the Millennium Development Goals and so halve absolute global poverty by 2015.

We call on Christians everywhere to be agents of hope for and with the poor, and to work with others to hold our national and global leaders accountable in securing a more just and merciful world.

All 191 members states of the United Nations have promised to achieve the Millennium Development Goals by 2015, a series of measurable, time-bound targets addressing poverty and hunger, education, maternal and child health, the prevalence of diseases including HIV and AIDS, gender equality, the environment, debt, trade justice and aid.

> **FACE FACTS**
>
> It has been estimated that for each of the 24 million people who signed the Jubilee 2000 Debt campaign petition, more than £4000 of debt was cancelled. Social spending across all Highly Indebted Poor Countries is estimated to have risen by about 20 percent. Mozambique was able to introduce a free immunization programme for children and primary school fees were abolished in Uganda, Tanzania, Zambia and Malawi.
>
> Source: The Micah Network

You can play a vital role, by inviting your group, your friends and your church to sign the Micah Call. If you are also a leader or a member of a Christian organization, network or denomination, you can help by asking your organization to formally sign the Micah Call.

● **Sign on paper:** you can print off the Micah Call from the CD-ROM (*Resource 10C: Printable*) or download a printable Micah Call sign-on sheet, to collect signatures at church and other gatherings, from their website www.micahchallenge.org/ index/National_Campaigns.asp.

● **Sign on-line:** you could e-mail people you know using some suggested wording, or write to them in words of your own, asking them to consider signing the Micah Call.

Globally – in the mean time (20–60 mins)

As you think about returning this book, and the issues it covers, to your shelf it is essential that your conclusion includes some form of commitment to take seriously your responsibility toward the poor and your, and the group's, role in a different world. In order to do so you'll need to consider where you've come from, where you are now and where you need to begin, as you start to make tangible plans to ensure you and your group see a much different world in the future.

| PAST | ← | PRESENT | → | FUTURE |

Whether you chose to do the following 'exercise' as a whole group or as the leaders of your group is your choice. Rather than cramming it into an existing session, you may feel it more appropriate to set aside a separate session. A meal, or a reflective study on a passage such as John 13:1–17 (see page 91), may provide just the right kind of environment to enable you to evaluate, to set targets and to think through areas of potential change in a non-threatening, informal and yet significant way.

1. RECALL YOUR FEELINGS

Return to the thoughts you had about a different world during the first session, by once again recalling your response to the question 'What is poverty?' If you feel you need to, display some of the images and sticky notes from the initial exercises or take another look at the video *'What is Poverty?'* (*Resource 1B: Video*). Ask your group to summarize their initial response to question 'What is poverty?' before they began to think through the issues in more depth.

> **HELPFUL HINT**
>
> The original definitions of poverty probably referred to hunger; lack of shelter; not being able to read or go to school; being sick but not being able to see a doctor; not having enough money to pay the rent; living one day at a time; or powerlessness.
>
> Poverty is not having the choices many of us take for granted.

2. REVIEW YOUR EXPERIENCE

In pairs, ask people to try to write a sentence which they now feel best defines poverty. Encourage positive rather than negative statements, i.e. without words such as: 'lack of', 'not', but instead with words that speak of a hope for a different future. Revisit some of your initial thoughts on your role in a different world. In what ways have your attitudes changed? Where you are now, where were you, and where do you want to be over the coming weeks, months, years, particularly in terms of:

● Your relationship with God

● Your relationship with the group

● Your relationship with the people with whom you share this different world with?

3. RESPOND THROUGH YOUR ACTION

Either by referring back to the poverty gap exercise in this session, or picking one of the major issues from a previous session, encourage your group to discuss small lifestyle choices that they feel they could make in order to bring about bigger life choices to others: locally, nationally and globally, for example a commitment to support a project working with the poor, an overseas trip, regular giving. In order to ensure your ideas stand any chance of fulfilment, it is probably advisable to try to categorize them into the following steps, setting realistic timescales and specific action points to ensure they happen:

● SHORT TERM i.e. in the next few weeks

● MEDIUM TERM i.e. in the next few months

● LONG TERM i.e. in the next year and beyond.

A DIFFERENT AIM
POVERTY — NOW YOU DO!

Jesus was a change-maker. Throughout his life and ministry, he impacted people's lives, not only through his words but through his actions too. The question is: can we?

Not everyone who dismisses God is disillusioned with him directly: many people are disappointed with Christians who say one thing and do another. In Jesus we see an example of someone whose 'words, works and wonders' are able to exist together comfortably and without compromise. His words of freedom, challenge and correction were backed up by his acts of justice, compassion and consideration. In turn, through his healing, his words of knowledge and his ability to listen to the marginalized, he demonstrated he was a God of wonder and not just a God of works or words.

If we want to become people who bring about change, people who make history, who 'see God's kingdom come', then when we demand change we need to be able to demonstrate that we, too, are prepared to make a commitment to make changes in our lives to further the cause. Take a look at John 13:1–17, a classic example of a God who acts and then says, 'Do likewise.'

KEY QUESTIONS

- How would you feel if Jesus knelt to wash your feet? How would your reaction have been similar to/different from that of the disciples?

- Why was it important that Jesus did what he did? Why didn't he just tell the disciples what to do?

- In what ways could this kind of model impact your life, your group, your wider community and beyond?

- What kind of decisions do you think you ought to make about your own life before calling for change in the way others make decisions?

Read, pray and reflect. Jesus never asked anyone to do anything that he wasn't prepared to do himself. If we are to bring change to our world – globally, nationally and, of course, locally – it's a lesson we need to learn.

Recognize that the world is hungry for action not words. Act with courage and vision. (Nelson Mandela, speaking for Make Poverty History, *Trafalgar Square, February 2005)*

DIFFERENT LINKS
USEFUL CONTACTS

TEARFUND

Tearfund is an evangelical Christian relief and development agency working through local partners to bring help and hope to communities in need around the world. The purpose of Tearfund is to serve Jesus Christ by enabling those who share evangelical Christian beliefs to bring good news to the poor.

NETWORK

This provides youth leaders with resources, support and advice on how to tackle issues of justice, poverty and integral mission with their groups. Network's FREE magazine, published three times a year, includes biblical reflection, in-depth articles, easy-to-use session plans and practical ways to express faith at local, national and global levels.

ACTIV1ST

Tearfund's FREE bi-monthly magazine for 11–17-year olds.

UNCOVERED

Tearfund's FREE termly magazine for students and young adults.

TRANSFORM

A short-term opportunities programme – your chance to work alongside Tearfund partners in the UK and overseas. Options include, **Transform...**

● **International**: 2 weeks, 4–6 weeks or 4 months (18+)

● **Yourselves**: Tailor-made UK and overseas projects for groups (14+)

● **UK**: 2 weeks working alongside inner city churches (16+)

● **Year Team**: 2 days a week working for Tearfund, 2 days working for a placement church or community project in the UK and a day studying or working.

To find out more about Tearfund...

Visit: www.tearfund.org/youth
E-mail: enquiry@tearfund.org
Phone: (+44) 0845 355 8355
Write to: Tearfund, 100 Church Road, Teddington, Middlesex TW11 8QE, England

CLIMATE

Energy Saving Trust is one of the UK's leading organizations tasked with sustainable energy solutions in homes and on the road. To find out more...

Visit: www.est.org.uk
Phone: 020 7222 0101
Write to: 21 Dartmouth Street, London SW1H 9BP

Friends of the Earth inspires solutions to environmental problems which make life better for people. To find out more...

Visit: www.foe.org.uk
E-mail: info@foe.co.uk
Phone: 0808 800 1111
Write to: Friends of the Earth 26–28 Underwood Street, London N1 7JQ, UK

Green electricity means electricity produced from sources which do not cause negative impacts upon the environment. Of course, every type of electricity generation will have some impact, but some sources are much greener than others. The cleanest energy sources are those which utilize the natural energy flows of the Earth. These are usually known as renewable energy sources, because they will never run out. To find out more...

Visit: www.greenelectricity.org

Recycle-More is a one-stop recycling information centre. You will find help and advice on all aspects of recycling at home, at school and in the workplace. To find out more...

Visit: www.recycle-more.co.uk

Sustrans is a charity that works on practical projects to encourage people to walk, cycle and use public transport. To find out more...

Visit: www.sustrans.org.uk
E-mail: info@sustrans.org.uk
Phone: 0845 113 0065
Write to: National Cycle Network Centre, 2 Cathedral Square, College Green, Bristol BS1 5DD

Transport 2000 is the independent national body concerned with sustainable transport. It looks for answers to transport problems and aims to reduce the environmental and social impact of transport by encouraging less use of cars and more use of public transport, walking and cycling. To find out more...

Visit: www.transport2000.org.uk
E-mail: info@transport2000.org.uk
Phone: 020 7613 0743
Write to: Transport 2000, The Impact Centre, 12–18 Hoxton Street, London N1 6NG

WATER

WaterAid is the UK's only major charity which is dedicated to the provision of safe domestic water, sanitation and hygiene promotion to the world's poorest people. To find out more...

Visit: www.wateraid.org
E-mail: wateraid@wateraid.org
Phone: 020 7793 4500
Write to: WaterAid, Prince Consort House, 27–29 Albert Embankment, London SE1 7UB

CONFLICT

Amnesty International is an independent worldwide movement working toward the universal recognition and practice of the universal declaration of Human Rights. To find out more...

Visit: www.amnesty.org.uk
E-mail: information@amnesty.org.uk
Phone: 020 7033 1500
Write to: Amnesty International, 99–119 Rosebury Avenue, London EC1R 4RE

Control Arms is a campaign jointly run by Amnesty International, IANSA and Oxfam. To find out more...

Visit: www.controlarms.org

Peace Brigades International (on invitation) sends teams of volunteers into areas of repression and conflict, in order to accompany human rights defenders, their organizations and others threatened by violence. To find out more...

Visit: www.peacebrigades.org
Phone: 020 7324 4628
Write to: Peace Brigades International, Unit 5, 89–93 Fonthill Road, London N4 3HT

ASYLUM

Churches Commission for Racial Justice was set up by the British and Irish Churches so that they could engage in issues of race and justice together. It is a part of Churches Together in Britain and Ireland. To find out more...

Visit: www.cix.co.uk/~ctbi/ccrj
E-mail: ccrj@ctbi.org.uk
Write to: Churches Commission for Racial Justice, Inter-Church House, 35–41 Lower Marsh, London SE1 7SA

Committee to Defend Asylum Seekers. To find out more...

Visit: www.defend-asylum.org
E-mail: info@defend-asylum.org
Phone: 07941 566183
Write to: CDAS, BCM Box 4289, London WC1N 3XX

Enabling Christians in Serving Refugees (ECSR) group seeks to resource, support and encourage Christians who practically support (or would like to practically support) asylum seekers and refugees in either a voluntary or professional capacity, while linking up asylum seeker and refugee support and befriending initiatives across the UK. To find out more...

Visit: www.ecsr.org.uk
E-mail: ecsr@welcomecentre.org
Phone: 020 8778 7788
Write to: ECSR, The Welcome Centre, 105–107 Maple Road, London SE20 8LP

National Coalition of Anti-Deportation Campaigns (NCADC) is a voluntary organization that provides practical help and advice to people facing deportation on how to launch and run anti-deportation campaigns. To find out more...

Visit: www.ncadc.org.uk
E-mail: ncadc@ncadc.org.uk
Phone: 0121 554 6947

Refugee Highway Partnership is a network of the Mission Commission of the World Evangelical Alliance. Its aim is to strategically support the process of building collaboration among churches, NGOs and ministry teams for greater long-term ministry effectiveness. To find out more...

Visit: www.refugeehighway.net
E-mail: hub@refugeehighway.net
Phone: ++1 604 628 3480

Student Action for Refugees (STAR) is a unique organization giving university students and young people the opportunity to learn about and raise awareness of refugee issues in innovative ways, and support refugees in a practical way in their local communities through volunteering and campaign with and for the rights of refugees everywhere. The STAR network is made up of university based student groups, young people (16–18-year olds) involved in the STAR Youth Programme and Friends of STAR (individuals and organizations who support the work of STAR). To find out more...

Visit: www.star-network.org.uk
Write to: STAR (Student Action for Refugees), 3 Bondway, Vauxhall, London SW8 1SJ

The Refugee Council is the largest organization in the UK working with asylum seekers and refugees. They not only give help and support, but also work with asylum seekers and refugees to ensure their needs and concerns are addressed. To find out more...

Visit: www.refugeecouncil.org.uk
E-mail: info@refugeecouncil.org.uk
Phone: 020 7346 6700
Write to: Refugee Council Head Office, 240–250 Ferndale Road, London SW9 8BB

HIV AND AIDS

National Aids Trust (NAT) is the UK's leading HIV and AIDS policy development and campaigning organization. NAT works in the UK and internationally for policies that will prevent HIV transmission, improve access to treatment, challenge HIV stigma and discrimination, and secure the political leadership to effectively fight AIDS. To find out more...

Visit: www.nat.org.uk
E-mail: info@nat.org.uk
Phone: 020 7814 6767
Write to: National Aids Trust, New City Cloisters, 196 Old Street, London EC1V 9FR

Stop AIDS Campaign is an unprecedented initiative of the UK Consortium on AIDS and International Development, bringing together more than 70 of the UK's leading development and HIV and AIDS groups. Launched on World AIDS Day 2001, the campaign works to raise awareness in the UK about the global HIV and AIDS epidemic and to campaign for urgently scaled up international action. To find out more...

Visit: www.stopaidscampaign.org.uk
E-mail: info@stopaidscampaign.org.uk
Phone: 020 7253 5860
Write to: Stop AIDS Campaign, c/o UK Consortium on AIDS & International Development, New City Cloisters, 196 Old Street, London EC1V 9FR

UNAIDS is the Joint United Nations Programme on HIV and AIDS. It is the main advocate for accelerated, comprehensive and coordinated global action on the epidemic. UNAIDS' mission is to lead, strengthen and support an expanded response to HIV and AIDS that includes preventing transmission of HIV, providing care and support to those already living with the virus, reducing the vulnerability of individuals and communities to HIV, and alleviating the impact of the epidemic. To find out more...

Visit: www.unaids.org
E-mail: unaids@unaids.org
Phone: +41 22 791 3666
Write to: UNAIDS 20, Avenue Appia, CH-1211 Geneva 27, Switzerland

TRADE

Equal Exchange is a fair trade company supplying a range of fair trade food and drink. To find out more:

Visit: www.equalexchange.co.uk
E-mail: info@equalexchange.co.uk
Phone: 0845 345 4889
Write to: Equal Exchange Trading Ltd, 10a Queensferry Street, Edinburgh EH2 4PG

Fairtrade Foundation exists to ensure a better deal for marginalized and disadvantaged producers in poor countries. The Foundation awards a consumer label, the FAIRTRADE Mark, to products that meet internationally recognized standards of fair trade. For more information on products, suppliers, resources and how to get more involved...

Visit: www.fairtrade.org.uk
E-mail: mail@fairtrade.org.uk
Phone: 020 7405 5942
Write to: Fairtrade Foundation, Room 204, 16 Baldwin's Gardens, London EC1N 7RJ

Fairtrade online. Fair trade foods and crafts from Oxfam and Traidcraft. To find out more...

Visit: www.fairtradeonline.com

Tearcraft is Tearfund's fair trade business. Tearcraft exists to benefit skilled artisans from some of the world's poorest communities, helping them to create and market products of the highest standard and ensure that a fair price is paid for their work. For a catalogue...

Visit: www.tearcraft.org
Phone: 0870 240 4896

Trade Justice Movement links organizations concerned with the negative impact of trade on the world's poorest people and the environment. They work together to put pressure on the UK Government to take the lead in international negotiations to change the rules for better. To find out more...

Visit: www.tradejusticemovement.org.uk

Traidcraft has the UK's widest range of fair trade products. For a catalogue...

Visit: www.traidcraftshop.co.uk
E-mail: help@traidcraft.co.uk
Phone: 0870 443 1018
Write to: Traidcraft Plc, Kingsway, Gateshead, Tyne and Wear NE11 0NE

Lift the Label is Tearfund's ethical lifestyle campaign for students and young people. For more information and resources on ethical food, fashion and finance...

Visit: www.tearfund.org/lifthelabel
E-mail: enquiry@tearfund.org
Phone: 0845 355 8355
Write to: Tearfund, 100 Church Road, Teddington, Middlesex TW11 8QE

DEBT

Jubilee Debt Campaign (JDC) is the UK's campaigning successor to Jubilee 2000 and Drop the Debt – a coalition of regional groups and national organizations whose focus is on changing UK Government policy on debt and influencing the policies of the World Bank and International Monetary Fund. To find out more...

Visit: www.jubileedebtcampaign.org.uk
Phone: 020 7324 4722
Write to: Jubilee Debt Campaign (JDC), The Grayston Centre, 28 Charles Square, London N1 6HT

AID

Disaster Emergency Committee is an umbrella organization uniting 13 of the UK's major aid agencies, which launches and co-ordinates the UK's National Appeal in response to major disasters overseas. Its members are: ActionAid, British Red Cross, CAFOD, CARE International UK, Christian Aid, Concern, Help the Aged, Islamic Relief, Merlin, Oxfam, Save the Children, Tearfund and World Vision. To find out more...

Visit: www.dec.org.uk
Phone: 020 7387 0200
Write to: Disaster Emergency Committee, 15 Warren Mews, London W1T 6AZ

[1] Make Poverty History. www.makepovertyhistory.org

[2] National Aids Trust. www.nat.org.uk

[3] Jubilee Debt Campaign. www.jubileedebtcampaign.org.uk

[4] These figures are based on research conducted as part of Tearfund's Lift the Label campaign. Visit www.tearfund.org/liftthelabel for more information.

[5] Make Poverty History. www.makepovertyhistory.org

[6] UNHCR, the United Nations Refugee Agency. www.unhcr.ch

[7] United Nations. www.un.org/documents/ga/docs/51/plenary/a51-306.htm

[8] Institute of Civil Defence and Disaster Studies. www.icdds.org

[9] Dewi Hughes & Andy Atkins, *Overcoming Poverty: Tearfund's Understanding* (Teddington: Tearfund, 2004)

[10] Such as the World Bank, UN, International Monetary Fund and the World Trade Organization.

[11] *Summary for Policymakers, a report of Working Group I of the Intergovernmental Panel on Climate Change* (January 2001)

[12] *Summary for Policymakers*

[13] *Summary for Policymakers* and Dinyar Godrej, The no-nonsense guide to climate change (2001)

[14] International Federation of Red Cross and Red Crescent Societies, World Disasters Report 1999

[15] *Summary for Policymakers*

[16] *Summary for Policymakers*

[17] *Lifesaver* leader's guide (Teddington: Tearfund, 2001), p.14

[18] *Lifesaver* leader's guide

[19] *Before Disaster Strikes*, Tearfund report (28 October 2000)

[20] Tearfund, *A Tearfund Guide to Climate Change: global warming* (Teddington: Tearfund, 2001)

[21] *Summary for Policymakers*

[22] World Wildlife Fund. www.wwf.org.uk.

[23] Energy Saving Trust. www.est.org.uk

[24] www.est.org.uk

[25] www.est.org.uk/solar

[26] Energy Saving Trust – an independent body established by the government to provide free advice to households, businesses and public sector bodies on how to save energy.

[27] Good Energy (formerly known as unit-e). www.good-energy.co.uk

[28] For more information call Good Energy on 0845 456 1640, e-mail enquiries@good-energy.co.uk, or visit www.good-energy.co.uk. By quoting UE38 if you switch they'll donate money to Tearfund.

[29] Rethink Rubbish. www.rethinkrubbish.com. Recycling your organic waste is the most efficient way to reduce the main source of methane emitted by landfill sites.

[30] UK Greenhouse Gas Inventory, 1990 to 2001. *Annual Report for submission under the Framework Convention on Climate Change* (July 2003)

[31] Waste online. All landfill sites that contain organic biodegradable material will produce 'landfill gas', which is typically composed of 60 percent methane and 40 percent carbon dioxide, and is normally saturated with moisture. www.wasteonline.org.uk

[32] See note 29.

[33] www.rethinkrubbish.com

[34] Energy Saving Trust. www.est.org.uk

[35] Organizations involved in offsetting emissions include Future Forests (www.futureforests.com) and Climate Care (www.climatecare.org). Costs range from about £7 to offset the carbon dioxide emissions from a short flight (e.g. London to Lisbon return), to £15–20 for a return trip to South Africa, and £40–50 for a return trip to Australia. For more information on being a responsible tourist visit: www.tearfund.org/tourism.

[36] Details of routes near you and free maps can be obtained from Sustrans on 0117 929 0888 or visit www.sustrans.org.uk.

[37] World Health Organization (WHO) and United Nations Children's Fund (UNICEF) (*Global Water Supply and Sanitation Assessment*, 2000).

[38] The UN Millennium Development Goals are eight targets agreed by all 191 members of the United Nations (UN) designed to halve world poverty by 2015. The goals are to eradicate extreme poverty and hunger, to achieve universal primary education, to promote gender equality and empower women, to reduce child mortality, to improve maternal health, to combat HIV/AIDS, malaria and other diseases, to ensure environmental sustainability, and to develop a global partnership for development. Visit www.un.org/millenniumgoals to see how we are doing and for a further explanation of each of the goals.

[39] *WaterAid News* (25 March 2005). www.wateraid.org.uk

[40] World Health Organization (WHO)

[41] WHO

[42] Department for International Development (DFID). *The Rough Guide to a Better World* (London: Rough Guides, 2004), p.32

[43] *WaterAid News*, 25 March 2005. www.wateraid.org.uk

[44] Unicef/WHO

[45] According to Severn Trent Water, every bath you take uses about 110 litres (when filled to a depth of 20cm), whilst for every five minutes you're in the shower you use 30 litres of water. Power showers can use between 15 and 60 litres of water every minute! www.stwater.co.uk

[46] www.stwater.co.uk

[47] Bryan Evans, *The Costly Game: A study of the arms trade and development* (Teddington: Tearfund, 2001), p.5

[48] Control Arms. A campaign jointly run by Amnesty International, IANSA and Oxfam. www.controlarms.org

[49] Amnesty International

[50] Amnesty International

[51] UNHCR, *Internally Displaced Persons: Questions & Answers* (Geneva: UNHCR Media Relations and Public Information Service, 2004)

[52] The Refugee Council

[53] Supporter Information Sheet: *UK ASYLUM SEEKERS* (Teddington: Tearfund, January 2004)

[54] *The New Internationalist* (October 2002)

[55] National AIDS Trust

[56] UN 2004

[57] Stop AIDS Campaign

[58] Stop AIDS Campaign

[59] UN 2004

[60] UNAIDS

[61] Stop AIDS Campaign

[62] Fiona Pimlot, Tracy Roslyn and Peter Wylie, *Sex* (Oxon: BMS, 1998), p.49

[63] UNAIDS

[64] UNAIDS. http://womenandaids.unaids.org. According to UNAIDS, young women and girls are more susceptible to HIV than men and boys, with studies showing they can be 2.5 times more likely to be HIV-infected as their male counterparts.

[65] Phil Bowyer, *Express Community: Bringing Social Action to Life* (Milton Keynes: Authentic Media, 2004), p. 21

[66] CAFOD, 2003

[67] Department for International Development. www.dfid.gov.uk

[68] CAFOD, 2003

[69] CAFOD 2003

[70] CAFOD. www.cafod.org.uk/get_involved/campaigning/campaign_issues/trade

[71] Make Trade Fair. www.maketradefair.com

[72] Trade Justice Movement

[73] Fairtrade Foundation. www.fairtrade.org.uk/get_involved_fairtrade_towns.htm

[74] Jubilee Debt Campaign. www.jubileedebtcampaign.org.uk

[75] These countries are: Cameroon, Chad, Democratic Republic of Congo, Gambia, Guinea, Guinea Bissau, Malawi, Sao Tome Principe and Sierra Leone.

[76] Although a further 15 countries – out of the total of 42 – are classified as Heavily Indebted Poor Countries and therefore eligible for debt relief under the HIPC initiative, only seven of these are thought likely to reach the first stage and receive any debt relief: Burundi, Central African Republic, Cote D'Ivoire, Comoros, Congo, Myanmar and Togo. The remaining eight are unlikely to ever reach this stage: Angola, Kenya, Laos, Liberia, Somalia, The Sudan, Vietnam and Yemen.

[77] Jubilee Debt Campaign

[78] These countries are: Benin, Bolivia, Burkina Faso, Ethiopia, Ghana, Guyana, Honduras, Madagascar, Mali, Mauritania, Mozambique, Nicaragua, Niger, Rwanda, Senegal, Tanzania, Uganda and Zambia. www.jubileedebtcampaign.org.uk

[79] These countries are: Cameroon, Chad, Democratic Republic of Congo, Gambia, Guinea, Guinea Bissau, Malawi, Sao Tome Principe and Sierra Leone. www.jubileedebtcampaign.org.uk

[80] See note 87.

[81] www.jubileedebtcampaign.org.uk

[82] Only four EU countries – Denmark, Sweden, Luxembourg and the Netherlands – have achieved the target, which was set 35 years ago.

[83] Simon Jeffery and Jon Dennis. The Guardian (10 December 2003). http://money.guardian.co.uk

[84] Department for International Development. www.dfid.gov.uk

[85] Disaster Emergency Committee. www.dec.org.uk

[86] Department for International Development. The Rough Guide to a Better World (London: Rough Guides, 2004), p.32

[87] Marshall, Millard, Packer and Wiseman. New Bible Dictionary (Leicester: IVP, 1996)

[88] UN Human Development Report 2002

[89] UN Human Development Report 2002

[90] UN Human Development Report 2002

[91] UN Human Development Report 2002

[92] UN Human Development Report 2002

[93] UN Human Development Report 2002

[94] UN Human Development Report 2002

[95] UN Human Development Report 2002

[96] UN Human Development Report 2002

[97] UN Human Development Report 2002

[98] UN Human Development Report 2002

[99] UN Human Development Report 2002

[100] UN Human Development Report 2002

[101] UN Human Development Report 2002

[102] UN Human Development Report 2002

[103] UN Human Development Report 2002

[104] International Coffee Organisation

[105] Fairtrade Foundation

[106] UN Human Development Report 2002

[107] UN Human Development Report 2002

[108] UN Human Development Report 2002

[109] UN Human Development Report 2002

ALSO BY PHIL BOWYER:

EXPRESS COMMUNITY

This is an inspirational and practical guide to give young people the methods and principles needed for social action. In order to be effectively equipped it is essential to spend some time looking at the Bible and working out exactly what needs doing.

Each session includes Bible study, prayer opportunities, responses, games, activities and ends with a practical application and step-by-step instructions to put what you've learnt into practice.

It ends the debate that evangelism and social action are two separate things and enables you to develop a more purposeful approach to serving Jesus in your community.

'Full of gems...I thoroughly recommend Phil as a writer whom I respect and admire...an excellent resource.'
Pete Hughes, Soul Survivor UK

'My young people are eager to get out and do some stuff in the local area. I can see this being a great resource to capturing some of their drive and turning it into vision and focus.'
Mark Massey, Youth Co-ordinator for Rayleigh Baptist Church

'Packed full of insight, inspiration and some of the best session material any group is ever likely to need...a handbook to action that takes the truths of scripture and translates them into a manifesto for service.'
Nigel Roberts, YFC

Phil Bowyer is Tearfund's National Youth Specialist. After training as a youth worker at the Oasis Youth Work and Ministry course, he spent five years as a youth worker. Phil is a regular speaker at Spring Harvest in the Evolution programme.

Written for leaders and members of groups aged 12 to 30

ISBN: 1-85078-583-X

Available from your local Christian bookshop